The Truth About Building Muscle

Mental Muscle Book

By Jeffrey Bedeaux

The Truth About Building Muscle

Table of Contents

Detailed Table of Contents

Introduction

About this book

Hello and welcome! Thanks for purchasing my new e-book. It's loaded with revolutionary proven knowledge and techniques that will allow you to quickly and efficiently transform your body to whatever level of fitness and muscularity you desire. You can do muscle toning or firming or conditioning for a sport or **even adding 20, 40, 60 pounds of new, hard muscle** to your frame. All without drugs and without spending a fortune on nutritional supplements and without wasting your time in the gym.

You see, a while ago my 25-year-old friend told me was getting into lifting weights at the gym and he wanted to know what I thought he should be doing in the gym to maximize his results. He knew that I wrote books on the subject, performed research on trainees from 16 to 82 years of age, measured the results every step of the way and synthesized them into full workouts and specialization workouts. He knew all that and more but he didn't want to read that much, he just wanted his best friend to tell him the core knowledge from all those books and all that research. The best of the best without any preamble, padding myself on the back or self-serving BS about how smart I was compared to others. So I gave it to him. Nothing more; nothing less.

That made me realize I really could condense what I've learned developing new data, feedback from customers, and experience from personal consultations. Everything into a book that I could make available to anyone in the world via the Internet.

And that's what you have right now. The best information garnered from years of research in real world testing. I urge you to read every word of it. The knowledge you need is in these pages and is laid out in a concise format and I don't repeat the same things over and over. That is with the exception of safety. Safety is the most important piece of information you can get out of this book. With that said I wouldn't dwell on it too much.

Getting the most from this book

If you are like most guys, you're tempted to turn to the chapters on workouts and dive right into your workouts with those killer techniques and principles. That's because most muscle heads see bodybuilding as merely hoisting weights up-and-down, over and over, slowly increasing the weight, under some misguided concept of this is what builds muscle. These are the guys who are always on the lookout for the magic routine that has eluded them for so long. Don't make that mistake!

Now I know you're not going to like to hear this, but read this manual all the way through before beginning your program. I want you to get on the gym floor in the quickest time possible but I want you to be armed with the advanced knowledge needed to put that time to good use. If you skip a chapter thinking you already know everything needed to know about that training factor, you could be setting yourself up for a big disappointment. But don't worry I'll be there every step of the way.

We will be covering a lot of information in this book. Information that is anything but common knowledge even among the professional bodybuilders who rely on anabolic steroids for their massive gains. Well, there you have it. I've sufficiently warned you of the dangers of skipping ahead in this book and I've given you a couple of "extra emphasis" tools to make sure you get the most important details from all information I have jammed into these pages.

Also, you will notice a couple of inches of open space at the bottom of each page; I did this for a reason. I want you to write down and highlight the most important parts for you. This open space is for your notes. By reading and writing the ideas that really connect with you, you will be able to absorb and use those points without even being aware of it. Print out this book and write all over it; I want you to squeeze every benefit out of the huge amount of information within these pages.

Two other tools you will see throughout this book that will help you understand the key points are *The Doctor Says* dialog box and the *Doctor's Prescription* dialog box. Look for boxes like these as you are reading:

The Doctor Says:
"Look here for insights into the topic being discussed."

Doctor's Prescription:
Look in these boxes for action steps you can take.

These 2 dialog boxes will help you get the most important information first. Also use them as a guideline for writing your own notes at the bottom of each page. After you have read this book you can skim through it later and read only the dialog boxes and your personal notes to re-connect with all the information contained in this book. I have found this technique to be very valuable to me when I want to skim a book I have already read and review the key points.

So here's what I want you to do now. If you have already been busting your ass in the gym training three to four days or more per week. Take a week off! You'll understand why later, but for now just plan on using that week to review this manual and fully prepare for your fiery return. If you're relatively new to bodybuilding, or it has been awhile since you've been in the gym, take the next week to introduce your body to what it's about to experience. In order to avoid overloading your body to the point of shutdown it's wise to begin a light exercise routine to prepare your muscles, joints and ligaments for the upcoming barrage. You don't want to go all out to the point you can barely move the next day. That would defeat the whole purpose of the first couple weeks of this program. Besides if you're looking for is an intense workout session, the real workout is coming up.

Dedication

This book is dedicated to every bodybuilder and athlete who has an acquiring rational mind; to every person who can throw off the chains of comfortable habit and unproven premises and move into new direction that is guided by reason and observational evidence, no matter where that direction takes him; to every person to try something immediately and thinks "How can I make this better?" To every person who is unafraid to challenge the false beliefs of the herd and lead others out of the cave and into the light.

In the world of bodybuilding it is these people with these genetics who are truly the greatest champions of the human race. To these people not just in the science of human strength but also in every science we all owe our enormous gratitude.

Why an e-book?

Some people ask me why I wrote this as an e-book. I could have written the draft of this book and taken to a mainstream book publisher, but there are a few reasons why I self-published this as an e-book and they all benefit you.

Freedom of content: E-books can contain links to related material, special pages or even built-in programs. Also big publishing companies don't like controversy. They don't like writers being too blunt about certain topics. They prefer to re-edit or re-word certain things. With an e-book, which I both write and publish, I conclude whatever content I want to include. Which leads me to....

Freedom of style: Any writer does better when he uses his own "voice". For example, in a mainstream publication I would have to say, "many professional bodybuilders use dangerous drugs to augment their muscular development." But in my own e-book I can say, "pro bodybuilding is filled with unbridled use of every type of drug imaginable.

Steroids represent less than 10 percent of what drugs bodybuilders actually use today. The full truth is that they use up to 20 prescription drugs at the same time and 1000% of the recommended safe dose. They take drugs intended for diabetes, cancer, dwarfism, pain, bloating, cardiology, hematology, impotence; the list goes on and on.

Athletes and regular folks are dropping dead every year and the huge meltdown is coming because the real health effects (tumors, heart failure, kidney failure, etc) appear to take at least fifteen years to show up. Soon we'll be hearing about the failing health of the great names of bodybuilding from the '80s and '90s, if you haven't heard already." Try finding that kind of plain talk in a nice mainstream book. I'm sure you won't find it especially if the author puts down supplements anyway since that's where the real cash cow is in bodybuilding.

Freedom from templates: Mainstream publishers have a formula they have to follow. It is just the realities of the book business. Right now is the larger book format (9" x 11") with approximately 220 pages; it is all about shelf space in the bookstores and perceived value. So a new e-book with about 120 pages loaded with new ideas that's guaranteed to put 40 pounds of muscle on you doesn't have a prayer of getting into print, but a 220 page book showing women doing "workouts" with 3 pound dumbbells gets in every bookstore and featured every woman's magazine.

The perception of what is valuable is very different from what really has value in the gym. An e-book format allows me to get right to the point without adding a bunch of filler, such as lots and lots of pictures that you have already seen, to get the book up to 220 pages.

The amount of information packed into this e-book took 17 years to determine and compile. It can unlock the greatest muscle growth you've ever experienced. When Einstein writes $E=MC^2$ on a piece of paper, it doesn't take a many pages but that knowledge can unlock enormous power.

Freedom of marketing: Digital content and the Internet is the wave of the future in publishing. When a mainstream book is published it gets an initial marketing push by the publisher and then it's all done. E-books can be promoted by links, banners, affiliate programs, and "word of mouse" that keep it in front of bodybuilders every day. Why should you care about that? The financial success of this e-book fuels the next one and that brings you more useful research information instead of the crap that's available in many books. As you can see in the bookstores, mainstream publishers say the same thing day after day, year after year.

Freedom of access: Less than 5% of the world's population lives in America. It can be pretty difficult and expensive to get an American book delivered to Turkey. But an e-book can be delivered around the world without extra costs and you can be reading it 20 seconds after you buy it.

And I'm not talking hypothetically here; this e-book not only sold copies in the United States and Canada, it also sold in the United Kingdom, France, Germany, Sweden, Switzerland, Australia, Brazil, Ireland, Singapore, South Africa, Denmark, Malaysia, China, Japan, Belarus, American Samoa and the Netherlands. All in the first 60 days!

Like the bodybuilders in the above countries around the world you're about to discover this e-book is absolutely loaded with useful information you can apply in your next workout. You're literally minutes away from the most productive workouts of your life.

Why I wrote this book

First let me explain why I wrote this book, I'll phrase it into a short story were I'm sure you can identify with the main character.

Let me introduce you to Average Joe. Joe is very typical of the bodybuilders trying to pack on muscle in today's gyms. Determined to look like "the huge guys" in the magazines, he signed up for his membership at the local gym, buys his weightlifting gloves and belt and all the other "essential tools" for packing on the pounds, and begins his quest.

At the gym he follows the lead of all the other "muscle heads" and begins bench pressing, curling, and squatting the most weight he can. Like the other misinformed Joes, he thinks that working harder and harder, steadily increasing the weight on the bar will force his body into growth beyond his wildest dreams. He makes some gains; enough to keep pushing on but soon finds himself stagnated.

Not seeing any more strength or size development Joe decides to go to the next level. He looks around the gym for the biggest iron pumping "consultant" he can find that also looks friendly enough to talk to. That guy is The Juice. Joe approaches Juice to inquire about the secrets to his bodybuilding. Juice tells Joe everything he knows about what exercises to choose, how much weight to use, what to eat and what "super supplements" to use.

Joe sets out again following everything Juice tells him; positive he now has the missing links to maximum growth. Some of what Juice told Joe was enough to move him out of his plateau temporarily. Within a few weeks he finds his strength and size stalemated again.

Frustrated Joe decides to turn to the "experts". He goes to the local bookstore and picks up every bodybuilding magazine they have and begins his research. Obviously with arms and legs the size of telephone poles and a chest the size of 2 Webster's dictionaries, anything these pros have to say must be gospel. Then there all the ads for the top-secret supplement discoveries promising you God-like powers from all the "latest" scientific research.

Confused and frustrated Joe spent a small fortune on supplements and is back in the gym. He is loaded with tips from all the pros and has so many "secret potions" running through his veins that he can be declared off-limits as a toxic waste dump! He makes a small gain, only to find it wither away as he hits "the wall". The wall is the place that all beginning and novice bodybuilders hit when they realize that building muscle is a whole lot harder than those hulking professionals in the magazines make it look.

Now comes the moment of truth. Here are the facts.

Fact: All those pro bodybuilders trying to coax you to purchase the next wave of natural supplements guaranteeing massive growth, got that big not from the natural supplements they are marketing but rather by pumping massive quantities of anabolic steroids into their veins.

Fact: The killer pre-contest and mass building routines those pros let you in on are enough to throw any bodybuilder into chronic overtraining without the aid of a serious dose of dangerous growth hormone and steroids. Or make you sick from a depressed immune system or seriously injure yourself.

Fact: The bodybuilding supplement market is a multi-multi-million dollar industry that is supported by well-intentioned serious seekers of muscle and fitness such as yourself, fall prey to the ads and articles designed for one thing, to take your hard earned money.

Fact: Supplement manufacturers and gym owners all follow the six-month rule of marketing. Basically six months is how long research has shown it takes the average "seeker of strength" to join a gym, purchase the supplements they're convinced they need, reach the wall where they see no more gains, get frustrated, and quit their workout program.

Fact: Those same bodybuilding magazines that projected air of "objectivity" actually own many of the supplements they're advertising and are recommending in their magazines.

Here are some of the worst offenders:

Flex: Weider Supplements
Muscle & Fitness: Weider Supplements

MuscleMag: Muscle Tech
Muscular Development: Twinlab
Muscle Media: EAS

These companies weren't stupid. They realized early on that they could sell you a magazine full of great looking perfectly sculpted columns of muscle to make you feel puny and weak; then offer you ad after ad of expensive supplements with pumped up scientific claims to milk you for even more of your dough.

Be careful

Caution: This program involves a systemic progression of muscular overload that leads to lifting extremely heavy weights. As a result, a proper warm-up of muscles, tendons, ligaments, and joints is mandatory at beginning of every workout.

Warning: As this is a very intense program, it requires both a thorough knowledge of proper exercise form and a base level of strength fitness. Although exercise is very beneficial, the potential does exist for injury, especially if the trainee is not in good physical condition. As always consult with your physician before beginning any program of progressive weight training or exercise. If you feel any strain or pain when you start exercising, stop immediately and consult your physician.

A look at the human mind

We realized that the mind has the ability to advise the body and that many bodily functions are actually signals from the brain, which is the life support system for the mind. We also learn that thoughts are subtle forms of energy. And that everything that is manmade came originally from a thought.

Can you see thoughts?

Now consider for a moment the material world around us, including our bodies. What is the cause of all that we see? Contemplate who it is that observes and notices all the things around us. Who is that invisible I inside our bodies?

If we examine ourselves and out of this state of investigation we look at, what is most important in our life; Trust, Honesty, Peace, Freedom, Loyalty, Respect, Confidence, Courage, and Humbleness. To most of us all of this is very important, yet very invisible or unseen. Even love goes unseen unless followed by action. So what is really important to some of us, are the invisible, unseen, immaterial, no-things in life; and many times in our lives these no-things become more important than our some-things.

This is the beginning of our understanding of spirit. The spirit has a thought, which created the mind; the mind has thoughts, which created the body. The spirit is the foundation; this unseen world is the source of all that is visible.

Let's observe ourselves scientifically and we will discover that we are not our own creation. Let's go back to conception, as one drop of human protoplasm, colliding with another, resulting in the form of an embryo and then there you evolved. If you turn up the magnification in the microscope and look further into that human protoplasm you'll find atoms, electrons, sub-atomic particles; then further magnification you'll find vibrating waves that come and go, these waves are mostly unseen. The source of all is therefore no-thing since it is not in the dimension of the measurable.

Your own creative abilities originate in the unseen mind. In the unseen world of waves and energy called thoughts. So what has all this to do with health?

Many of us try to exercise daily, join a gym, start jogging and lift weights. And some of us actually try to eat properly and try to stay away from abusive habits. However, it seems that with the majority of us, the gym and the good nutrition is short lived. In my experience, 90 percent of the people never make it to the eighth week. Some four percent last up to six months, make wonderful changes, but then go back to poor habits and non-attendance when it comes to exercise.

Without the involvement of spirit, consistent exercise, correct nutrition and positive thinking are very short lived. Very few have inspiration in the spirit. Spirit gives you strength when your mind and body gives up. **Spirit is what separates the genius from**

the ordinary. Spirit is what creates champions. No need to look up; look within, it's right there, invisible and unseen.

What happens within your body everyday

Your body is made of 60 trillion cells, or 60,000 billion. Think of this number. Each one of these cells carries out the necessary work required to sustain life. Each cell uses up and regenerates oxygen. Each cell has its own climate control, producing moisture; it has its own farm of amino acids, vitamins, minerals, glucose and fat.

Each cell has its own power and waste recycling plant. Each and every day 8 million of your body's cells dies and 8 million are created to replace them. Your body contains 100,000 miles of blood vessels (veins and arteries). This distance is equivalent to traveling around the entire earth four times or half way to the moon.

Every day your heart beats 100,000 times. Each time pushing new and re-oxygenated blood through each and every inch of your blood vessels, then back again to your heart, every day. Your heart requires only 60 pumps to complete one entire trip. Your heart continues this work every second of every day for some 80 plus years, or the rest of your life.

Along with that, each heartbeat inserts the correct amount of oxygen into every one of those 60 trillion cells within your blood, along with disposing of waste contained within them. Along with oxygen, food, energy and essential nutrients are deposited into each cell, which is then again transported throughout the body.

Now imagine how much harder this work would be for your heart if you didn't exercise; high cholesterol and fat clog arteries. With all this going on in your body it still maintains a temperature of 98.6 degrees.

What about when you cut yourself? Of course, your body naturally heals the wound, but can you imagine how much work it is to repair this? How does your body know how to do all of this work? Your brain carries out all of these functions, most of which you are never aware. Nobody ever teaches it how to do this work. Yet from the first miraculous day of conception your brain is able to carry our every one of these infinite numbers of operations, with pinpoint accuracy that cannot be altered, otherwise you would die.

It would take the world's fastest computers hundreds of years just to be able to scan what our own eyes see in one day. This miraculous body of yours, with all of its wonders, is able to go off and produce another human being from scratch. It builds a new miracle cell by cell. Once completed, this new life is sent out into the world with all of the necessary instructions to make it grow and build into an adult. Once you become intimate with this knowledge you may experience divinity within.

Mind over matter

Your mind is the most powerful weapon you have. You can imagine a maximum of power developing inside yourself day by day and your weak points getting eliminated. You can feel more energy and a great pump.

The transition of approach in bodybuilding is a great aspect as bodybuilding has thousands of techniques and concepts. The very important element is transition of mind and body. We can see that transition in mind and exercise beginning from the very first day of training. One who starts exercising feels the new change in his body for the first time. As he feels his muscles and tendons are getting stretched and blood getting pumped in his body he feels new every minute. This real feeling changes during every new day of exercise and when a beginner trains for weeks he will feel much change and improvement in his body and mind.

After a proper training of more than a year his entire view about iron sport will change and shall continue to change by the passage of time because experience is the best teacher. All this will create a great transition. After following much new modern principles of training a bodybuilder can change his entire training program from every angle. Training and very top nutrition opens new horizon in mind and soul, as one gets strong. His mental thinking changes continuously. This is a great angle of bodybuilding that as long as you continue it, it changes humans' abilities continuously if continued with great spirit.

So the transition of mind forms great transformation of body after a strong period of struggle. Transformation is an ultimate wish of every bodybuilder and it requires the ultimate concentration of mind and soul together with great effort in training. The mind over matter is an interesting fact. For example, if you are trying to push 250lbs of weight on the bench and you are not making it, but after few minutes you somehow get inspired and your mind suddenly gets ready for the push then your muscles will follow too and you be able to push the weight to some extent. For very quick transformation of a body into pure ultra-muscular and powerful body your mind and soul's seriousness and concentration will play a great role because your body will follow the command of your consciousness.

In bodybuilding one thing must never be forgotten and that is to go for the maximum. Never think of less. You should train and eat at high extents but with some limits too.

One step at a time

Like in real life you take one step at a time; this idea also applies to bodybuilding. Each step you take you must understand the philosophy behind your training and nutrition, as your greater understanding will create your transformation because your body will follow what your heart will follow. **Positive thinking is the best thinking.** You should always think of doing the best and try for the best and you must not think of less or depression. People might say to you that "hey you don't have a nice body yet," but this sentence must not be taken as real and you should work the best to achieve the ultimate growth. As there are always infinite capacity of growth present in your mind and body.

Setbacks may occur in life and also in bodybuilding and you may feel great loss of health but this does not mean you should stop. You should always continue with great exuberance and ultimate struggle towards excellence in bodybuilding. This can yield super results. In very clear meaning, **the ultimate transformation of body will take place when you will stimulate your mind and body to extreme levels but with one**

step at a time because this will make the base of your physique strong from deep within. Follow your instinct and create your own programs, which suit you completely. For ultimate growth perform the training with highest acceleration in mind and power. Bodybuilding is just not about making muscles, it teaches you a variety of techniques on various aspects and approaches in life. It increases your courage and willpower and much more. The art is very deep; so always step forward not backwards.

The Doctor Says:
If you are going to take bodybuilding seriously you have to use the power within your mind. This is where your true power lies.

How the mind builds the body

Would you like to remain always young, and would you carry all the joyousness and buoyancy of youth into your mature years? Then have care concerning but one thing, — how you live in your thought world. This will determine all. It was the inspired one, **Gautama, the Buddha, who said, — "The mind is everything; what you think you become."** And the same thing had Ruskin in mind when he said, — "Make yourself nests of pleasant thoughts. None of us as yet know, for none of us have been taught in early youth, what fairy palaces we may build of beautiful thought, — proof against all adversity."

And would you have in your body all the elasticity, all the strength, all the beauty of your younger years? Then live these in your mind, making no room for unclean thought, and you will externalize them in your body. In the degree that you keep young in thought will you remain young in body. And you will find that your body will in turn aid your mind, for body helps mind the same as mind builds body.

You are continually building, and so externalizing in your body conditions most akin to the thoughts and emotions you entertain. And not only are you so building from within, but you are also continually drawing from without, forces of a kindred nature. Your particular kind of thought connects you with a similar order of thought from without. If it is bright, hopeful, cheerful, you connect yourself with a current of thought of this nature. If it is sad, fearing, despondent, then this is the order of thought you connect yourself with.

If the latter is the order of your thought, then perhaps unconsciously and by degrees you have been connecting yourself with it. You need to go back and pick up again a part of your child nature, with its careless and cheerful type of thought.

The time will come when the work of the physician will not be to treat and attempt to heal the body, but to heal the mind, which in turn will heal the body. In other words, the true physician will be a teacher; his work will be to keep people well, instead of attempting to make them well after sickness and disease comes on; and still beyond this there will come a time when each will be his own physician.

In the degree that we live in harmony with the higher laws of our being, and so, in the degree that we become better acquainted with the powers of the mind and spirit, will we give less attention to the body, — no less care, but less attention.

The bodies of thousands today would be much better cared for if their owners gave them less thought and attention. As a rule, those who think least of their bodies enjoy the best health. Many are kept in continual ill health by the abnormal thought and attention they give them.

Give the body the nourishment, the exercise, the fresh air, the sunlight it requires, keep it clean, and then think of it as little as possible. In your thoughts and in your conversation never dwell upon the negative side. Don't talk of sickness and disease. By talking of these you do yourself harm and you do harm to those who listen to you. Talk of those things that will make people the better for listening to you. Thus you will infect them with health and strength and not with weakness and disease.

Never affirm or repeat about your health what you do not wish to be true. Do not dwell upon your ailments, nor study your symptoms. Never allow yourself to be convinced that you are not complete master of yourself. Stoutly affirm your superiority over bodily ills, and do not acknowledge yourself the slave of any inferior power. . .

No man's success or health will ever reach beyond his own confidence; as a rule, we erect our own barriers.

Mental strength

It's one thing to be physically strong in the gym. It's another to be mentally tough also. This can make all difference for a person. The biggest guy can be made to look the smallest if he doesn't have it upstairs, and vice-versa. I'm not talking about book smarts or knowing the square root of 169. **I'm referring to mental confidence and maintaining focus in the gym.**

Arnold Schwarzenegger once said that you have to walk into a gym like you own it, no matter if you're the biggest guy or one of the smallest guys. This doesn't mean walking into a gym and running your mouth to everyone. Let your body and body language speak for you. Stand up straight, chest out, and head held high. Don't slouch with your shoulders rolled forward while staring at the ground. Walk like a big guy, even if you're not. Trust me; people will definitely look at you differently. You would be surprised at how many people are more concerned with who is around them than they are with what they are doing.

Try to avoid that pissed off look that some people strive for; you'll just make yourself look like an asshole. Some people think that by looking like this, that they will intimidate others. Most people can recognize this as a front anyways. I've always gotten a lot of criticism outside of the gym for not talking to anyone, even my friends or family, while I work out. So what, why would I talk? It doesn't make any sense to me to walk into a gym like it is some social event. It takes work to build up intense concentration and even more work to maintain focus, so don't risk losing that. You can walk into a gym and talk with your buddy or something, but after you pick up your first weight, then it's all business. There is plenty of time in the day to talk all you want before and after a workout. If you really feel like you have to talk, and then bring a MP3 player with music that will get you going. I've found that a MP3 player will increase your ability to keep your focus. In addition, you need to keep a workout log, which will both keep you busy, and keep track of your progress. One time, I walked into the gym with a MP3 player and a hat pulled down. No one recognized me. It was great! It was like I was working out in a new gym. Not even my friends knew who I was.

The Doctor Says:
To make the best gains, keep the socializing to a minimum while you are working out. Talk to your friends before or afterwards.

Avoid grunting or yelling while you work out. This will make you look both retarded and hungry for attention. Truthfully, I'd rather my workout partner yell at me or count my reps loudly. That's another thing, if you have a partner, you will be able to hold your focus, and you'll be able to compete with someone in order to make yourself work harder. You get some critics, but who cares, just work hard and appreciate it.

Like I said, avoid talking shit to anyone, and let your actions speak for you. If someone comes up to you after your workout or whenever, don't be a butthead. It takes a lot for someone to ask for advice from a total stranger. I've never believed in acting like an ass to someone who may know a little less than you about working out. **Give back because somewhere down the line, someone helped you out too. There's a fine line between being confident and arrogant, try not to cross that line.**

Now, when you're out of the gym, don't talk to all of your friends about working out. You'll look like a complete idiot and a muscle-head; you can disregard this if you're talking with a fellow muscle-head. There's nothing worse than a single-minded person. I try to avoid talking about the gym outside of the gym. Let others know that there is more to you than just dumbbells.

Beware, there's always that one person who will come up to you while you are training and say, "Why do you do that exercise?" in a condescending tone. There are a couple of things you could do. You could be a prick and say "Shut the hell up, I'm trying to work out!" or you could just say, "Well, it works for me." I'd go with the latter, don't be a hot-head if someone comes up to you and tries to question you during your workout. Believe it or not, you'll find that same person coming up to you asking for advice later on.

Remember, walk confident, don't grunt/yell, don't be a hot-head, and no conversing during the workout. Above all, have fun!

Mental tools

What saves the seasoned veteran from "choking" during the heat of competition? Why is it that you never seem to keep your concentration? No matter how hard you try you can't seem to stay focused. Can you get too pumped up? Why it is the young man in football, with less talent, works harder to earn a starting spot? While another player, with far more talent, sits the bench? These are just some of the questions plaguing us today in this highly competitive world of athletics.

Transforming barriers into boosters

You know what they are; we all have them. Mental barriers, blocks, and fears! Call them what you may, but they are correctly titled momentum barriers. Why? Well, because these momentum barriers only side bar your drive and continual progress in any athletic training endeavor. Any barrier, if approached the right way can be broken down. Even if the barrier is solid steel, there is still a way to make that barrier crumble. It is important for you to keep your attention focused on going to the gym, executing each exercise, each rep and getting everything you are supposed to do each and every day. If I let the disappointment of not getting the correct number of reps and sets outlined for that exercise then I would have got upset, gone home and pouted. Like I am sure most of us have done when things don't go our way.

Hey, there are going to be days when you will walk in the gym and then walk right back out. But not because your friends wanted to go hang out somewhere or party. No, but because physically your body needs a rest. Does this mean you're going to fail, or does this mean you're not going to reach your goals and you're not mentally strong? No, not even. **Everyone's body needs a rest.** But, off-season rest doesn't mean to go off and forget everything until the last minute either. That's what separates the best from the rest. Getting prepared for the season is a lot different than beginning of a season practicing football, baseball, volleyball, basketball, wrestling, or any other competitive sport.

As an athlete, you should know when you're down and dirty into the last weeks of preparation for the season and it is hard to get up and practice. This is when you need to dig deep into your mind. Place a word in your head that will always motivate you. Think of the other team, what are they doing? What is your opponent doing right know? What about those goals we set out to accomplish at the beginning of this season? That's it! That's all it takes, a few different ways to shake up your head.

Everything in moderation

I know this is bordering on bodybuilding blasphemy but for those of us who aren't clinically insane this is something that has to happen. Moderation does not mean dropping back on the training sessions, or the intensity. **Moderation in weight training means not making the gym the focus of the day.** If your day revolves around your trip to the gym, then you are lining yourself up for an overdose. Some people prefer to hit the gym in the afternoon, and some prefer to hit while they are fresh in the morning. My advice is to try and become a morning person. Hit the gym early and be pumped for the rest of the day. If you prefer the afternoon workout, leave it as late as possible, so you can back it up onto dinner after a couple of hours.

The Doctor Says:
Moderation in bodybuilding means that you are keeping yourself out of an overtrained state. Moderation is training frequency is the best way to accomplish this.

Secondly, keep your training sessions short and sharp. 45 minutes is a good length, and is attainable if you keep focused and keep the recovery time away from excess. Once you start going over the hour mark, you start to lose focus and your workout will lose its effectiveness. These points seem to be really straightforward and common sense and they are. In fact, they make so much sense that most people are oblivious to their necessity. So remember:

- **Do not revolve your life around the gym**

- **Try be a morning person**

- **Keep it under an hour**

Have a life

This can end up being a big problem for amateur bodybuilders and often results in giving up their regular lifestyle. And don't kid yourself, bodybuilding is a lifestyle. If you want to get serious about what you are doing, there are whole ranges of factors you have to consider, from nutrition to sleeping patterns. The problems arise when you start slapping the "burden" label around and you end up complaining about the lifestyle.

Bodybuilding is just another way of living

It's not better, its not worse, it's just different. You can look at each aspect and label them "benefits" or "downfalls" but essentially it is just another way of living. Being a bodybuilder does not restrict you from fun. If you are living a serious bodybuilding lifestyle and you can't have fun then you aren't trying. Work your program so you can get away once in a while, and always keep friends close by. Don't take yourself too seriously and work each aspect of who you are into your lifestyle.

Do you think bodybuilding is restrictive on your personal life? Well you are wrong. Arnold, Coleman and all the other big names were not hermits by any stretch of the word. I'm throwing the word balance around here because without balance you are asking for trouble. Organize yourself. Lifting and living do not have to oppose each other. The points to remember:

- **Bodybuilding is just another way of living**

- **Have fun**

- **Learn how to balance**

Use your rest and recovery time wisely

A good bodybuilder always gives himself space. When you feel it is time to change programs, it is a good time to take a week or more off to give your body some breathing space. Go someplace relaxing. This is not the time where you get smashed every night and crawl around hung over in the morning. This is where you expand yourself and do something different. Just don't exert yourself. Don't get unfit, but just do not break any world records. Here are some suggestions that are guaranteed to refresh the most worn out:

- **Read books.** Why do people not read anymore?

- **Go to the beach.** Nothing like surf and sand to kick out the jams.

- **Spend some time with the opposite sex.** This can be very relaxing.

- **Do something creative.** Take a couple of days to write an article.

- **Lie in the sun, hit the sauna, spa it up.**

- **Keep away from controversy.** Don't get fed up with the drama.

If you want to maximize your workout then work your mind as well. Do not fall into the traps that are so easy to ruin all the hard work that you put into shaping your body.

- **Keep things in moderation.**

- **Have a life.**

- **Use your R & R time wisely.**

If you want to keep pumping hard, then keep your life in balance, and understand that your mind is out to get you. Train hard, train smart.

<u>Building the mind of a champion</u>

So here now are the 12 principles to help you develop the mind of a champion. And I'll tell you; this is serious stuff for serious bodybuilders.

Enjoy and prosper from applying every one. And as you do, you'll readily appreciate what's involved in coming to stand victoriously atop Muscle Mountain's peak!

Pre-workout mental priming

Here, you stimulate your nervous system with the kind and quality of effort you want to generate while you train. Before your workout, clearly 3-dimensionally visualize yourself performing one set for each of the muscles you'll be training. And experience yourself generating super-human effort; pushing yourself, driving yourself, contracting to the max, and blasting ever fiber to the bone. Take your time here; each time you perform this process, your visualizations will become more lifelike, and positively emotionally activating.

Pure mental isolation and focus

This type of concentration is not the traditional type where you try to block out external distractions. Laser concentration is entirely different. It entails mobilizing all of your consciousness into a singular focus point that you then project into, and sustain within, a particular task involvement (i.e., each rep of every set throughout your entire workout).

This concentration form, once mobilized, is so powerful, you're not even aware of yourself. You just sense an extreme energy force lasered directly into the specific muscle you're training. And this is an essential part of producing full muscular development; bringing a muscle to where its full size and shape potential ultimately becomes actualized.

It takes determined practice and application to develop this laser concentration. And here's how you can do it: with each set you perform, purposefully bring your whole consciousness into the specific muscle you're training. This means your whole visual focus, all your emotions, your imaginative focus, your willpower, and your exclusive action intent.

F-e-e-l this "all of you" then begin to work the muscle with each rep, sustaining this same laser concentration during the positive and negative parts of each rep. If you sense you're drifting, just gently bring this "all of you" back into the wholly locked-in dimension. Just the same as a cowboy would redirect a stray that wandered off from the herd. Keep applying this laser concentration principle, and in a short time you'll find it will become your natural mental inclination.

Performing this principle as outlined, you'll almost feel like you're filling the specific muscle you're training with a compelling power. And as you continue applying this principle, you'll be able to direct maximum mental intensity into the muscle you train each rep of every set. And imagine what kind of gains this will make for you!

Cultivating and applying the pain barrier breakthrough

Mastering the pain barrier spells the difference between realizing your full potential, and just being "good." Recall a decisive workout power memory; one where you were in the zone, going beyond your max, or training with an almost animal like passion and intensity. To a degree where it was as if nothing could or would deny you. When you've isolated this memory, imaginatively step into it, and into your body. And wholly f-e-e-l the exact feeling and sensations you did. And as you're feeling this, think of one word that, to you, represents you embodying this feeling.

Mentally exclaim it to yourself 5 consecutive times with passion, and conviction. Then, when you're at your next pain barrier threshold during a set, forcefully mentally exclaim this word so it's as if, as you silently repeat it, it "explodes" to fill all of you with its power. Then, go on to crank out 2 more reps!

Developing mind/muscle communication

Over the years, the champions have told me they felt as if they could control every muscle in their body. As if they had a sort of individual relationship with every single muscle group. And so here, in the evening, lay comfortably upon your back, close your eyelids down, and begin to focus upon a specific muscle. When you feel you've mentally connected with it, then imaginatively "talk" to it. Tell it what you're going to do to it your next workout, and what you expect of it in terms of exertion, performance, and growth. Mentally go into "lagging" body parts, and do the same thing; talk to these muscles like they're your employee and you're the boss. Continue on with this process, and you'll be surprised, even amazed at how your muscles will begin to respond!

Determine and connect with your performance workout emotion

Emotions are to performance what gas is to your car; the highest-grade octane enables your engine to perform at its peak. And if you think about the best workouts you've had; when you literally felt like a machine, and almost unconsciously blasted through set after set, coming to feel a worked sensation that was the way you'd like to feel after every workout. You'll begin to realize an important fact. The kind of emotion fueling these workouts produces the most demonstrable results for you.

So **recall the very last time you had a peak performance workout. Then imaginatively step into the picture, and into your body.** Then, think what you did then, feel what you felt, say to yourself what you did, and breathe as you did. When you're replicating all the preceding, clench your right fist hard, and think the word "Power" 3 times. Then, very s-l-o-w-l-y unclench your fist. Now you've formed a peak performance emotion anchor. And I want you to use it in the following way:

Before each set, clench your right fist hard, breathe as you did in your peak performance workout, and mentally, passionately exclaim your key word "Power" 3 consecutive times.

You'll feel your specific success fueling emotion filling you rapidly. Then, unclench your fist, and go on to perform your set.

Recite a.m. personal power affirmations

Most "ordinary" people start their day as an extension of their yesterday. The truly accomplished start each day with an empowering mental "breakfast". This "breakfast" consists of thoughts and ideas detailing what they'll do, why they can, and that they will! I encourage you to tailor your own individualized personal power affirmations. And as an illustration, here is a framework you can adopt:

"Today I exemplify power. I am strong in my thoughts; I think 'Yes I can; I'm supposed to triumph'."

"I remain wholly confident in my beliefs; I can do what I set out to, and take myself higher because I choose to."

"I am disciplined, determined, and dedicated in my pursuit of excellence, physical excellence when I work out in the gym and life excellence as I go through the various tasks and responsibilities of my day."

"There are things I can do better than anyone else. And today...I shall!"

Set specific outcomes for every set, and each workout

Do you honestly spend the overwhelming majority of your gym time involved in productive growth and strength increasing efforts? Or, do you "sort of, kind of" just go through the motions and feel "Ok; I did my workout today"? Purposeful effort produces purposeful results. And here, I want you to determine the following:

A.) What is the overall result you want to produce/experience from your workout in terms of feeling, sensation, workload to be accomplished, and degree of performance generated?

B.) What is each set to produce for you, or result in? What you'll do, how you'll do it, and the degree to which you'll do it?

The Doctor Says:
You need a roadmap to get where you want to go. Have a plan for each workout and achieve you plan.

You must know where you're going if you're ever to get there. And so, have a well detailed, specific result you'll strive for always in mind. This way, you have a progress stimulating reason to exert, and a personally advancing purpose to strive toward. No more "half-assed", "idle", "routine", or "mindless" effort. From now on, know your outcome, and then set about achieving it.

Embracing the "push it to the limit and beyond" attitude

Here, you begin to internalize the same kind of overall training attitude the champs instinctively embrace. And this revolves around the sentiment "Just good enough...isn't!" The new attitude here is "If I've done what I've done, I've done it; now I dig in and push myself beyond!" The workout impact of this attitude actualized is a natural tendency to push, strive, test, climb, and triumph.

Appropriately attempt heavier poundages, appropriately attempt increased reps, appropriately attempt forced reps, appropriately attempt super sets, tri-sets, and giant sets! As an aid to developing this attitude, here's a peak performance affirmation you can begin internalizing about one hour before you leave for your gym:

"Today I strive for more. Today I push myself higher and harder, striving to bring more of myself into every rep of every set, and make my muscles exert more feverishly than I ever have before. I never rest on my laurels; I ignite the flames of conquest passion and today, push myself to the limit...and beyond!"

Deep mental relaxation to promote sound, restful sleep

The volts of intensity you generate during your workouts must be balanced with emotional/neurological calmness so you can fully rest, and deeply sleep each night. As you know, your sleep period is essential for recuperation and growth. So here, you now purposefully unwind before getting into bed to sleep, mentally and physically.

First, lying comfortably, perform 6-8 release breaths. Inhale deeply through your nostrils, letting your stomach expand and distend. Then slowly, easily exhale through your mouth. Next, calm and relax your mind by focusing upon your breathing. And with each breath, imagine you're expelling a white mist. And mentally, silently repeat the words "relaxing now" with each exhalation, experiencing your thoughts calming down, and the muscles in your head, cheeks and jaw slackening completely.

Next, just visualize and allow the deeply soothing looseness and comfort you feel to easily flow into, and fill your entire body; all the way down to your toes. You'll quickly come to feel a pleasant "heaviness" and a comforting inner peace enveloping you. Then, just spend a few moments enjoying the inner calm you've produced. Now, you're ready to enjoy the deeply restful sleep that supports your muscular growth.

The ideal motivation principle

If you've ever seen something you wanted, something you felt you really wanted, every time you either saw it or it entered your mind, a feeling of drive to get it also flow through you. Whether it was a car, a suit of clothes, a certain female who caught your eye, a job you wanted. The objective of your desire so captivated your "want power"; you likely ultimately came to acquire or produce it, didn't you?

It's very similar with physical development. When you've clearly formed an impression of your overall desired physique, and you wholly believe in, and are deeply excited by it, it naturally motivates you to expend the energy necessary to ultimately achieve it. So, as you get into bed to sleep, begin to mentally visualize and experience the imaginative answer to the following question. "If I could have the kind of physique I truly wanted, what would this look like, feel like and be?"

Then, to the best of your ability, **wholly sensory envision what this looks like from the front, and the rear. And be sure to experience every cut, groove, peak, and striation connected to this ideal you.** After 6 minutes or so of this success ideal visualization, then just let this impression fade, and allow yourself to drift off to sleep. Continue doing this every night, and you'll find your motivation will stay invincible, and your physical training drive will never waver.

Embracing the resolve toward completion

Are you an "Ok; I did enough" person? Or, are you an "I will do all I set out to" personality? Let me tell you that those who truly reach their muscular peak are the latter type. They'll fully complete what they set out to, and will not tolerate, or settle for anything less. And this applies to adding one full inch to their arms, or 50 pounds to their max bench press, or carving a tight, cut, muscular etched waistline.

The Doctor Says:
Better yet, become an "I will do everything within my power" type of person.

Goals are to be fully achieved. Workout plans and strategies are to be fully completed and actualized. Self-structured and determined standards of performance are to be fully adhered to and honored. Always. Don't compromise yourself, ever. The results you'll achieve through applying this principle will more than justify your effort.

Independent belief, look within yourself

This last principle is a very important part in you going as high as you can. Here, you determine how big, strong, developed, accomplished, powerful, advanced, and physically evolved you can become. No one knows you like you do. If you choose to consider and believe in limitations, rest assured you'll experience, at best, partial life and muscular achievement.

But when you choose to say what's possible for you, and really mean it, that's when all your power will be generated toward making what you believe a fact. Hold your beliefs. Tightly embrace your vision of self and possibility. And train fueled by these ideals.

Now you have the 12 mental training principles you can apply to significantly bolster your training efforts and results. And I encourage you to use them as outlined, so you keep developing yourself. It's up to you now. No one can or will do it for you, but you. And through the 12 mental training principles detailed, now you can bring your full power into play. Go ahead; start applying these principles in your workouts, and your life. Then, you'll come to understand how to move yourself from ordinary to extraordinary!

<u>What you think is what you'll get</u>

Your mental images manifest in your physical world. Here are some questions you need to ask yourself:

1. How can you become lean, fit and healthy if all you think about is gaining weight and eating your favorite unhealthy food?

2. How can you possibly be successful if all you think about is failing or losing?

3. How can you possibly make more money if you focus on being in debt?

4. How can you possibly get a better job if your energy is spent thinking about how much you hate your current one?

My Mental Fuel (Fuel is energy) what you give energy to grows! My Mental Images (instant brief snap shots of yourself) My Thoughts (meditations of images) My Mental Pictures (complete life like scenes of yourself) My Choices (decisions) and ultimately My Actions (every physical movement). You see, in life, everything counts. Therefore you must count everything. Sow a thought, reap an action. Reap an action, sow a habit. Sow that habit, reap a destination!

You are where you are, right now at this moment, because of your consistent thoughts, images, and actions, which is the composite of your habits. From this day forward, if you want to change your future, you must change your Mental Fuel.

In order to achieve your ideal body, your ideal state of thinking, your optimum level of health and performance in all areas of your life you must change your mental diet. You must get rid of all negative, self-defeating and destructive material, conversations, unnecessary relationships, images in your home and workplace.

Replace negative thoughts with empowering images by changing what you read, what you watch on TV and the Internet. Change the music you listen to. If you're depressed and you want to get to a higher more invigorating state, don't listen to sad "poor me" drippy songs. Put on some high energy moving and grooving music. Put on what I call great memory music. You know, the music you played when everything in your life was awesome. Let your mind take you back there to that place. Soon you will feel powerful again.

You do this by asking yourself empowering questions. You are a unique individual. You have your own picture of success. If you don't... GET ONE! Find some quiet space and start asking and answering these questions. Print out this page and write out your answers in detail.

What does my ultimate picture of success look like? What can I do to feel successful today? What can I read, study, ingest that signifies success to me? What do I need to do to be successful? Who can (really) help me achieve my success? What are the first three things I am going to change to start my success process?

1.____

2.____

3.____________________________________
4.____________________________________
5.____________________________________
6.____________________________________

Never look back at your past mistakes. That's why they call it the past! You know what didn't work, you know where your strength is. Call upon it. Develop your own success program. Each of us has our own ideal image of success!

Start now. Go out a buy a magazine that reflect your destiny and only look in that direction. Forget your past, believe me, everyone is tired of hearing about it. Look to your future see your reaching, see your journey. We are all on a journey through this life... Maybe we will meet along the way. I hope I see you at the top!

Avoid negative thinking

Negative self-talk is a destructive habit and part of an essential defense mechanism that we often develop to protect ourselves. Many people end up talking themselves out of actions that may be scary or uncomfortable. "I can't do this" is really just a way of saying "I don't want to deal with the experience of doing this." We are all strongly influenced by our feelings, often determining how and what action we ultimately take. If the feeling is uncomfortable, negative self-talk results; then we often decide not to take any action at all.

Many people assume that if a past experience produced a certain result, there is nothing they can do to change that experience in order to produce a different result. "I've tried every diet there is. I know what I should do; I just can't do it.

Please understand that you can make the choice not to repeat old patterns of eating, non-exercise, and negative thinking. You have the ability to choose the emotions you have. If you don't like feeling guilty, frustrated, or doubtful, you can choose not to. You, and no one else, must decide what is comfortable for you. **In order to become successful at making healthy choices, you must avoid negative self-talk and start practicing positive thinking.**

Positive or negative self-talk plays a big part in your decisions. Be on the "look-out for negative self-talk and notice how it influences your choices; notice how it can negatively affect your efforts to change. For example, perhaps you've just returned from a week's vacation where you took a break from exercise and high protein eating. You tell yourself, "I feel so skinny. I'm back where I started." You feel guilty and frustrated. "I don't have enough will-power to start all over again. Maybe I'm just meant to be small." Feeling overwhelmed and discouraged, you give up.

First, reflect on the feelings you had before you decided to give up. You basically told yourself that the healthy habits you learned before your vacation were all for nothing and that you have to start over. Ask yourself if these feelings are reasonable. Are you really back to ground zero? Of course not. You accepted change and developed a new way of living; these skills are yours forever. The vacation might even have done you some good: everyone needs a break sometimes.

Otherwise, you might have felt deprived and not really enjoyed yourself. It's time now to tell yourself: "It felt good eating whatever I wanted and taking a break from exercising; I had a great time. But now I'm going to focus back on the healthy, active lifestyle I was enjoying before vacation. There is no reason to beat myself up; I'll just take it one day at a time." Now you can rethink your previous decision and take action that will move you forward towards more positive change.

As you begin to understand your reasons for negative self-talk, you'll find yourself recognizing it more and more quickly after it occurs. Eventually, as you practice, you'll be able to recognize and stop negative self-talk before it interferes with your decisions.

Doctor's Prescription:
Being positive isn't only for the followers of Tony Robbins. Your mind is the most powerful tool you have at your disposal so give it positive thoughts to work with instead of negative ones.

It is very important to practice positive thinking and to remind yourself that you're a worthwhile person whatever you do. **Try to consistently acknowledge that you are making positive changes to improve your health.** You should be proud of yourself. **Visualize yourself as capable, happy, and confident.** These positive feelings will help the process of change. Remember, there are bound to be times when you're feeling frustrated or depressed. Positive thinkers know that these feelings are valid, and they don't try to ignore them. Positive thinkers acknowledge and try to understand them, but they don't blame themselves for the conditions that lead to these feelings. Good luck, stay positive, and enjoy all the wonderful benefits of a healthy lifestyle!

Hypnotism is a very powerful tool

I think I speak for all serious bodybuilders, whether you have competition goals or you just simply want a better physique, when I say that we are all constantly brainstorming for a serious way to conjure mental power to aid us along our bodybuilding journey. Well, what if I told you that by using the following simple mental exercises daily, you could ultimately reach and surpass all of your bodybuilding and personality goals with ease, and continue to make excellent progress for years? Interested? Then I encourage you, read on.

Hypnotism, the way I see it can be defined as stimulating the subconscious mind to reach a high level of success, one that you couldn't do with your conscious mind alone. The brain is generally made up of three sections: the conscious, unconscious, and the subconscious.

Your conscious mind perceives and determines ideas and objects in everyday life; it basically compares things to one and other, and makes choices. Your unconscious mind is just a defense mechanism and protects the life of an organism. The subconscious portion is what we will be discussing, because it can be "tuned" to make your bodybuilding choices easier if you stimulate it properly. The subconscious mind does not have the ability to compare, determine or reason like the conscious mind does. If stimulated to send information back to the conscious mind, that thought will shape and be responsible for your behavior.

For example, there are many people who are afraid of dogs because of a previous negative experience with one, usually when at a young age. This is commonly an intense situation that is stored in the subconscious "memory bank" and determines the behavior of that person, in this case being cautious around dogs. Another example of hypnotism in action is when you dream about things or people that you enjoy in everyday life, or even when you have a bad dream about a previous experience.

Unlike the above examples used, **the subconscious can be honed and allow you to become a great bodybuilder, if you let it.** Every mind has an unbelievable potential for success if it is "massaged" by hypnotism. As much as you can believe and your mind can conceive, to that degree you will be successful and complete your goals. Here is a simple process called "the charter method", which I attribute all of my successful time training to.

It is very simple, **you just simply chart all of your desires and goals you wish to reach, and think of yourself as already having accomplished them.** In my personal experience, I find that 3 distinct sections work well. First, chart how you want to look. Vividly describe every detail of your physique, as long as it is attainable and not a goal that is set too high.

Example:

"I have excellent symmetry, sheer size and definition. My traps are big, thick and insert widely into my perfectly round sculpted shoulders. My anterior deltoids are big thick squares like slabs; medials puffed out to the sides so much it looks like they contain synthol. My rear delts are large enough to make my shoulders look like boulders. Altogether, my deltoids give the illusion of great width and complete muscularity. My chest is perfectly sculpted and thick. Upper, as well as lower mass, delt-pec tie in, and a noticeable crevice running down the middle to give them a large, square look. My back is very wide, thick and fans out like wings, obviously the largest muscles on my upper body. My arms are mounds of thick powerful muscle, biceps high peaked, triceps overflowing with mass, and bands of muscle lining my forearms, even my brachailis are visible."

Next, you must chart your desired personality traits such as confidence, faith, strength, determination, focus, willpower, etc. Maybe something like this for strength:

"I have attained unbelievable brute strength. I feel complete confidence as I increase my lifts with additional repetitions and poundages ritually, like clockwork. I experience a true feeling of power while performing exercises. I am pound for pound, the strongest guy around. I am consistently moving more weight with more reps and at faster, more controlled paces."

Concentration:

"I have attained true mind power, the ability to narrow my mind down to one single thing and concentrate for prolonged amounts of time. While working out, I display a true mind muscle connection with a calm and determined approach, testing the limits of muscular stimulation. I feel every burning accumulation of lactic acid, as well as the exact extension, powerful contraction as well as every individual muscle fiber and striation

ripping and tearing as I continue my sets. I fully exhaust the target muscle group providing maximum stimulation for growth. I remind myself how much I want to get bigger and stronger constantly throughout my workouts."

Pre-workout Mindset:

"I will move more weight for more reps and reach a new level of success, crushing previously set barriers. I will display true mind-muscle connection and completely exhaust the target muscle group, and move on."

Read your charter whenever you feel needed, such as when you wake up; feel tempted when something else comes along and of course before a workout. I encourage you to allow you bodybuilding experience to be excellent, soaring and fun.

See yourself win; a look at sports

We all know that to maximize your potential in the gym we have to work out, eat right and live a fitness lifestyle. However, the mind and its impact on training are often overlooked. Most of us realize that through the use of psychological techniques developed to improve athletic sports performance you can take your training to the next level, but exactly what are these techniques and how do we take advantage of them? Hopefully, this section will answer some of these questions and help you to understand some of these concepts and how apply them to your training.

Imagery and self-confidence

In sport psychology, confidence is defined as "the belief that you can successfully perform a desired behavior". **Sports psychologists have long used the technique of visualization to aid athletes for increasing their self-confidence, motivation, and reduce performance anxiety.** By applying mental imagery, you'll discover a multitude of resources that will aid you in increasing your training and game time performance. I am a stout believer in imagery to aid one's self-confidence, technique, and playing performance.

What is imagery? Well, first let's discuss what self-confidence is all about. Again too much self-confidence can be construed with a big ego. I know, here we go again with that damn ego thing. The first thing in building self-confidence is to measure your level of confidence. There are a variety of ways that you can measure your confidence level in order to gain an accurate assessment. Below is a list of suggestions for how to measure your confidence levels.

- **Get to Know Yourself** - Make frequent observations of your actions and write them down when in different situations. Whether those situations are good or frustrating, write them all down.

- **Identify Your Own Behavioral Patterns** - Recognize how you are behaving in the above situations (e.g., the way you interact with other people in the gym, how you act outside the gym).

- **Prepare Your Own List of Questions** - Ask yourself certain questions that can help evaluate your confidence.

• **Evaluate All Sources Of Information** - review your observation notes, question responses and workout information.

Before You Walk Into the Gym

• How confident are you on a daily basis?

• What are you thinking about?

After The Workout

• How well did you perform?

• What were you thinking about when you had a bad set?

• What we're thinking before and after you had a good set?

• How did you recover from a bad workout or set?

• Under what situations did you lack confidence?

Once your self-confidence levels have been measured, the next step in your performance momentum steps is to build that confidence up. **The best and most effective way to build your self-confidence is to use imagery, positive feedback, and surround yourself with positive people.**

• **Imagery** - By being able to see yourself perform successfully in your mind, you begin to gain confidence in your ability to be successful in reality. Create a realistic picture in your mind, got it? Picture exactly what you want to accomplish on the field or in training. Incorporate all your senses so you can feel, hear, and touch the image you're creating in your mind. Repeat the scene over and over in your mind. Make it real!

• **Positive feedback** - When communicating to your support crew and friends focus on the things you're doing well, the things you need to accomplish, and focus on success instead of everything you are doing wrong.

• **Positive people** - This is probably the other best confidence builder next to imagery. The people around you can make or break you. If you have individuals that are always down, bellyaching over the little things in life, being upset over this and that, and partying instead of working then you need to cut yourself loose from such individuals. Keep upbeat people that are interested in the same things you are, individuals who know what you are trying to accomplish and you will be filled with self-confidence and success!

Your training program should be written out on a daily basis and most importantly prior to beginning your training program you should establish short and long-term goals for yourself. Here are some other factors that you should take into account:

• **Set specific goals;**

• **Set performance goals;**

• **Always set realistic and challenging goals; but most importantly,**

• **Ink it, don't think it!**

Write down in a journal your long term and short term goals. Long-term goals are usually for six months, a year or sometimes as far ahead as two years. And short-term goals are daily, weekly and monthly attainable factors. Always write things down so you can see every day what you are trying to accomplish. This aids in the visualization tool also. A specific goal can be something like: at the end of the off-season you are going to drop your 40-yard dash time down 2 tenths of a second. A performance goal can be set as how hard your workout is every day in the gym.

Remember, to be realistic in your goal setting. Do not think you are going to bench 400 pounds at the end of six months when you are only doing 275! Set your goal at 315 or 325. And if you set that type of goal and accomplish more, then that makes it all the better.

But, in most athletic events strength and conditioning programs can aid you in your mental edge. This can be a constant mental and physical battle engaging the everyday effort of lifting, running and applying other sport specific drills. Every day you go off to the stadium and gym in search of that perfect workout, that perfect day in competition when everything comes together; the exact weight on each exercise, the feel of supremacy, the right move, the correct response and all the little things are all a necessity. We are all searching for that perfect day and there are some athletes that do have those days. A day when the mental momentum just carries on to each and everything that you do on the field.

When you are preparing for competition during the off-season this does not always happen. Why? Well, most of us think if we had a great day, then tomorrow we will have a better one. Thus, we expect the next day to just happen. And this is the first step in creating bad mental tools. You must focus on executing your everyday goals, e.g., the exact number of hours for sleep; preparing and eat each meal; take all your supplements and vitamins; and drink lots of water. I can go on, and on but you should get the point. Do not become consumed with performance or showing-off because for everyday peak athletic performance you should take a look at how you did things prior to getting to that point.

Pumping mental iron

There are thousands of theories, issues and ideas thrown around in the bodybuilding fraternity. There are programs to suit every need, and contingencies for every problem. Our individuality demands that no two programs are alike, and no set list of instructions will provide the same result. Motivation and attitude are a big part of all sports, just ask anyone in the relatively new profession, sports psychology. There are countless programs for the body, but what about that other muscle we need to exercise just as regularly? Has anyone ever really say down and pushed his or her mind to the limit? How can you expect your body to go to new heights, if your mind takes a back seat in the gym? I'm not talking about ineffective or uneducated training, or even lack of motivation. I'm talking about balance.

There are some people who seem to be able to focus on a goal and not waver for even a moment. There are some who set down the rules and dare themselves to step over the line. This can be the making of a champion. **Arnold missed his own father's funeral in** preparation for Mr. Olympia. **Cold heartedness or iron determination? A bit of both I think. Arnold was a success machine. Winning was his life and he was good at it. Nothing was too big a sacrifice.** But what about the rest of us mere mortals? What about those of us who wander from the path? How do can I keep fresh and ready for the pain that I love to put myself through in the gym?

Throughout history

Throughout history there are examples of great feats of physical prowess, situations where the mind has had to overcome the limitations of the body. The most well-known example is Phidippides, the Greek runner. Phidippides ran a total of 280 miles in 3 days, fought in a war, and then ran another 26 miles with news of a victory. He died shortly afterward from fatigue, but he accomplished a feat that is still unmatched today. Certainly athletes today are in much better physical shape due to scientific training methods. But Phidippides demonstrated incredible mental fortitude, above and beyond the average person.

How exactly does the mind overcome physical limitations? What allows some people the mental edge in life and in athletics to go above and beyond the norm? **Most athletes and coaches agree that winning is 90% mental. It all comes down to this; those that can overcome pain, physical discomfort, and psychological barriers will succeed.** Realizing the importance of the mental game, most elite athletes enlist the aid of sports psychologists to better prepare them for competition.

There are several methods that sports psychologists use. They often use a combination of clinical skills and non-traditional methods in their practice. In the past, the non-traditional methods were scoffed at for many reasons; the main one being a lack of scientific research in the field. In the past 2 decades, research has shown that without a doubt certain methods can propel an athletes' career to a higher level of achievement.

Using imagery to overcome obstacles

The most common non-traditional methods that sports psychologists use are imagery, controlling psychic energy, stress management, and concentration skills. These methods have become necessary skills for athletes to master if they are to bring their performance to an elite level. They are all designed to enhance the mind-body link and allow the brain to have more control over the body. By this I mean in terms of neurological functioning, rather than simple movement, things such as pain control, neural pathways (skill), and sensory intake.

Of the four methods, imagery is the most important tool that sports psychologists use. **Imagery involves an experience similar to a sensory experience, but arising in the absence of external stimuli.** It can involve any of the senses, not just visualization. Imagery is used to help athletes acquire or practice complex motor skills, to rehearse strategies to be followed in a particular contest, and to develop a greater sense of self-awareness.

The concept of imagery is not a new one. It actually began with reports from India that the yogis there were performing remarkable feats. The yogis did this by actually controlling their autonomic nervous system, a system we thought we had no mental control over. One of the most famous studies done was aired on PBS. The Swami Raja allowed himself to be placed in a tank with a five-minute oxygen supply while scientists monitored his vital signs. They found that he slowed his respiration and heart rate down almost two-thirds of what his normal numbers were. The Swami Raja was able to control basic physiological functions after years of imagery training.

The psycho-neuromuscular theory

There are two main theories that attempt to explain why imagery works. The Psycho-neuromuscular Theory postulates that vivid, imagined events produce the same neuromuscular responses similar to those of an actual experience. You have to take care to duplicate any emotions you may feel at the time and any background activity that will be going on, such as noise. It seems that the images in the brain actually cause muscular contractions so small that no movement actually takes place, but the pathway is utilized.

Symbolic learning theory

The second theory is the Symbolic Learning Theory. This theory says that imagery develops a coding system of movement patterns. Imagery creates a mental blueprint in the central nervous system. Most scientists like this theory better than the Psycho-neuromuscular Theory because not all studies have been able to show neuromuscular activity. They also like it because it uses the principle of positive reinforcement. Imagery helps an athlete break cycles of bad play by imagining good play without ever stepping onto the playing field.

Imagery programs consist of three phases:

- **Sensory awareness**
- **Vividness**
- **Controllability**

Sensory awareness

In sensory awareness training, the athlete manipulates past experiences into what they want future experiences to look like. To do this the athlete must first become consciously aware of every movement involved in a particular skill. The problem with this is most athletes have performed certain movements so many times they don't think about them anymore. They can overcome this by slowing down their movements and using mindfulness to develop greater awareness.

Develop vividness

The second phase is to develop vividness. Imagery will not work unless you can duplicate in your mind everything that is going on during a competition. The athlete must consciously be aware of what their coach would be doing, what the crowd is like, any smells in the air, and what the weather would be like. Once they achieve this, their imagery sessions will be so close to the actual experience that their mind can't help but lay down blueprints of the actual skill movements.

Controllability

Phase three is relatively simple. It involves controllability. The athlete must learn to manipulate their images to produce the desired outcome. To do this they must achieve awareness and vividness so that the experience seems real. It cannot just be an unconscious thought of what happens next. The athlete must be in the same mindset that they would have in an actual competition.

Other ways to teach imagery

There are a few other minor skills sports psychologists use to teach imagery. They work with the athlete on relaxation techniques, focusing on actually relaxing during the competition. **Such a skill is called relaxed attention, the athlete is still completely focused in the competition, but their breathing, heart rate, and etc. is close to normal.** Usually an athlete is in a high state of arousal during competition and that can detract from their concentration.

Understanding what your motivation and expectations are is also important to imagery. Having unrealistic expectations will only lead to disappointment. Many athletes desperately want success overnight. No amount of practice or imagery training will do that. By tailoring imagery programs to short term goals, but still keeping the long-term goal in mind, an athlete will avoid setting up mental blocks that they cannot overcome.

Likewise, it is important to know what your motivation is. An imagery program revolves around achieving a goal. That goal may be anything from fame to money to personal growth. Whatever the case is, the athletes driving factor must be a part of their imagery program.

Imagery alone will not make a champion. Athletes still have to spend hours in the gym and on the field and also employ some of the other psychological techniques at their service. Nonetheless, what was once thought of as parlor trickery is now an integral part of their training regime.

The power of visualization

So what is visualization and how will it take my training to the next level? Well, my friend, people you've known and looked up to have been using the power of visualization to transform their lives for years. These people include Dale Carnegie, Tony Robbins (the motivational speaker in the movie *Shallow Hal*) Michael Jordan and Frank Zane, among many others. These people, though only just people, have made huge impacts to our society because of what they've accomplished. Yet, we all have the ability to change the world, but it starts with ourselves.

Visualization is visualizing in your mind what you will achieve and accomplish. **It's seeing yourself with all the great things you want, doing all the things you hope to do.** The power of visualization is that once these images start to be repeatedly put into the mind, the subconscious takes over and can't discern what is real from what isn't, and you become what you're focusing upon. For instance, have you ever noticed how when you purchase a new car of a specific color, you suddenly start seeing many other cars of the exact same type and color? Those cars have always been there, but you just haven't put the importance of the car into your mind.

Doctor's Prescription:
Your subconscious mind is 10X more powerful than your conscious mind so use it to your advantage and employ the power of visualization.

Many people always ask me questions such as, "Why do bodybuilders develop such great bodies, yet I go to the gym quite a bit and don't attain the level of fitness the greats do?" I tell them of course there are many factors when comparing yourself to the greats, such as nutrition, the ability to train without outside stresses, genetics, motivation from peers, access to information and other factors. One of the most important factors which aren't widely understood by the common trainee has to do with the mind. A favorite quote of mine is "What the mind can believe, the body can achieve."

Many of the greats had supposed "great" limitations, yet they broke through them by believing and seeing themselves achieve their goals. They saw themselves in their minds as much bigger, more muscular, winning the competitions, and taking their training to the next level. Many bodybuilders have broken through their "mind plateau" if you will, by forcing their mind to believe which in effect changes them.

It has been proven, that what you put into your mind you become, but that is one of the many reasons those who push through the barriers take themselves to another level most people don't. Many years ago nobody thought that a 4-minute mile could be performed, but once one man achieved it, soon hundreds followed. The mind can be an extremely powerful tool, used for good or bad. The mind can make you are break you. Now that I've given you some food for thought, try the following exercise.

Each day before you go to work or school, sit down, take 5 deep breaths to stimulate that immune system, and **for 5 minutes visualize what you hope to look like, what poundages you see yourself lifting, and view yourself with everything you want to accomplish."** This technique is so powerful, yet the people that do it still amaze our society because most people don't know the technique, and don't have control over this area. The saying is true, "garbage in, garbage out."

If you focus on something enough, you will become it. This is one of the reasons many small guys eventually break goals that most people will never break. That is why many powerlifters lift extreme weights while most men gawk at the mere idea of lifting those poundages. The powerlifters are surrounded by other men who are lifting those weights, and they begin to believe they can do the same if these men have, which makes it true for them. The mind is a powerful tool, used for good or bad, it can determine what you will or won't become.

Focus and visualization

Now then let's say that you are a hopeful politician running for office. You are really some nothing sophomore in college who is dreaming of becoming a senator. Well, you can't go from a nobody to somebody that fast! You would have to do something like become a lawyer, win a bunch of cases, get involved campaign, draw up a platform etc.

It is the same with training and diet! Let's say that so are trying to put on some muscle, maybe for a bodybuilding competition, a modeling audition, an audition in the bedroom with your significant other or maybe just walking down the street. Geek to freak, scrawny to brawny does not go anywhere without a focused plan of attack and something at the top of the mountain that you want to reach. In keeping with the theme of someone who trying to be more muscular, let's say you want to look something along the lines of a Ronnie Coleman, or in the less genetically gifted area, a Russell Crow type build. Words that come to mind are muscular, sinewy, ripped, chick magnet. So what should you do?

Find a picture of one of them and post it somewhere where you will see it. Maybe at the bedside, on the fridge if you need to keep a sharp eye on nutrition. Second write down a general goal. I want to look like this guy ripped to the bone, huge pecs, granite like muscle, big biceps, chiseled abs, v-shaped back, sweeping legs, etc. Then after so trial and error with training you should write a focused plan of attack:

Workout 3-4 days a week, highlight which exercises and body part pairings are right for you as an individual, and train as intensely as possible. Aim to increase lifts by 5% every 2-3 weeks. Pay attention to protein, carbs and fat. The plan is really up to what you want to do. If your body is important enough you will do it. Your body is your own masterpiece!

Get focused

There has been a lot written about getting into the right mindset for growth. Visualization and affirmations are great for psyching yourself up before the workout. It's easy to stand in front of the mirror visualizing your biceps growing like mountain peaks, but it's not easy to maintain that mental image when Ali Landry's twin sister is doing her stretching regime next to you. So let's zero in on what happens as you actually get to the gym and how you can preserve that pre-workout psyche you worked so hard to achieve.

The problems that affect your focus

There are many variations, but most distractions boil down to a few basic categories:

- **Equipment problems**
- **Other people**
- **Yourself**

Equipment problems are physical obstacles that you can't ignore. Your favorite chest-press machine may have an "OUT OF ORDER!" sign on it, one of the only two 120 lb. dumbbells in the gym may be missing, and a team of powerlifters has swiped every 45 lb. plate around for their deadlifts. You get the idea. These are the toughest obstacles to overcome since you have to improvise instead of sticking to your carefully planned course of action. But it can be done, as we'll see later on.

Other people are more of an annoyance. This could be Mr. Hotshot and his three buddies have decided to monopolize a key machine for 30 minutes straight. The Ali Landry-clone I mentioned earlier or the gym serial talker who latches on to you and babbles until your ears fall off or you plug the hole with a dumbbell, whichever comes first.

Last but not least, it's good old poor planning on your part. This can be failure to eat a good pre-workout meal or something as simple as forgetting to bring your sweat-towel to wipe off the equipment after yourself. Or going to the gym at the busiest time of day.

The solutions to these problems

The equipment issue is best solved by always having a contingency plan. If a specific machine is out of order, you have an interchangeable, alternate exercise you can throw in without missing a beat. Just make a note in your training log and move on. That applies to pretty much anything; keep a backup for each exercise, so that you won't have to stop and think: "S—t, now what do I do?" That's one of the worst derailers of training focus there is.

Problems caused by other people require a more flexible approach. The contingency approach works for skipping or waiting out Mr. Hotshot and his crew, but Ali is tougher. Try timing your workouts to minimize the number of attractive females around. Early mornings are typically popular, while you usually find a lot less hot stuff at 8 PM and thereafter. A friend once suggested imagining she is your sister, which should help take the edge off things for most normal guys.

The solution to talkers is to bring your radio or portable CD-player and keep the music blasting through the entire workout. This also shields your sensitive ears from horrors such as Backstreet Boys and Bryan Adams that moronic gym managers sometimes subject their clientele to.

So what about the problems caused by your own darn self? Well, if you're the type who doesn't learn from your own mistakes, get a PDA that will do the job for you. If you have a workout planned for 3 PM, set the PDA to beep at 1:30 to remind you that you should eat a bowl of rice and some chicken. Then have another, recurring alarm go off at 2:30, when you should be getting ready to head out the door.

Other tricks and ideas

• **Get a reliable training partner.** The keyword is "reliable"; you need someone who will be there, every workout, with a positive, can-do attitude.

• **Focus on the pump, and maintain the pump throughout.** This will help keep your mind off the babes and in your muscles.

• **Keep your eyes on the ground or looking at yourself in the mirror** and avoid eye contact with anyone, from the moment you start until you finish.

• The last trick, which has proved devastatingly effective by a few people I've unfortunately seen, is **to not bathe for two weeks.** Machines magically frees up by them merely approaching, and not even the most hardcore talkers ever accosted these people. But if you have so much trouble focusing, you're considering this alternative, I recommend getting a home gym instead.

Maintaining focus example in the gym

As you walk into the gym your feeling pumped up and psyched up. It's leg day. That dreadful day where intensity is the rule and without it you might as well kiss those "tree trunks" in the making goodbye.

Have you done this before? You get in proper position under the squat rack after placing the weight pin. You're excited because you're going to try 10 more lbs. this week. Then you glance in the mirror and see a lifter near you using 60 lbs. more than you. Doubt begins to creep into your mind that you might never reach that high mark you've set. Wait!?! What is that, Backstreet boys are playing over that speaker and oh, those 2 hot girls from school are staring at me. Well, I'm going to do this set now. **Squats down and pushes back up*** AHHHH! Spotters help me! Thanks, I guess I'm just not ready for this amount of weight yet.

What a familiar story, and yet it still re-occurs every workout for most people. The focus you had going into the gym was shattered. Doubt crept into your mind about your ability, and you let the girls put pressure on you to prove something. The music took your intensity level down and broke your concentration when you identified it as being the latest boy band. But why have these things ruined your set?

The loss of focus is just as detrimental to your lifting gains as a bad diet. How many people do you know who have a decent diet and workout all the time, and yet they never go up in weight or gain a substantial amount of size? It's a tragedy, and it's happening to bodybuilding hopefuls and even happens to the heroes here and there. Years ago I was one of these people. No matter what my diet or training split was I failed to make substantial progress. This inability to gain was my entire fault.

The topic being presented is so very important to me because of the sheer magnitude at which your mental focus plays in your bodybuilding. I debate with many people about what true bodybuilding is, and even when diet and training is in place, most people over look this vital aspect of the bodybuilder package. Without it, you will never reach your potential because your mind is not yet strong enough to take you there. It is possible to develop the mental ability and strength that will drive you to the top, and I believe everyone can do it. We are made in God's image; there is nothing we cannot do.

Broken limitations

Once I broke the "limitations" and developed the focus needed, my bench immediately jumped 20lbs, and probably could have jumped 50lbs if I had more faith in my own potential. It took months for me to finally realize how important using the focus and drive I possessed in each and every workout was.

I spent years training like most people, lack luster and going through the motions. But over time I began to understand what true bodybuilding was, and the extreme effort and fatigue that goes into it. You might be wondering, "But Jeff, with all the people who trained back then, how come they could keep their intensity up for such periods of time?"

Well, it's actually been documented and said by many bodybuilders of the past that most of them trained no more than 1 hour per workout. Arnold, Draper, the list goes on, but much of what has been passed down has been exaggerated to make the legends appear greater. That is how it is with everything. So now that you have an idea about this intensity and mental drive, let's get down and dirty and see how we can help develop our own drive so we can have the best possible workouts every time we hit the gym.

If you want the best progress possible you need to develop gym mentality. So in a way I'm saying you need to "put on the blinders." **Let nothing around you seep into your mind during training.** You have to be a "man on a mission." You must believe nothing will stop you in the gym, and you are going to become a monster. See yourself growing and lifting huge amounts of weight that mere average men wouldn't dream of.

One tactic Greg Kovacs uses is when people stare at you just pretend you're putting on a demonstration for everyone in the gym! I've tried it, and it works wonderfully. When lifting, place your focus on the muscles you are working and see them growing. Anything to keep your intensity and focus directed towards your lifting.

Take a cd/mp3 player with you to the gym, and put that music that really gets your adrenaline going and takes your motivation through the roof. You know this type of music; it makes you want to be a hero. Imagine yourself where you want to be as a bodybuilder in the next several years, then on your way to the gym and inside the gym think of yourself as that person already. Your lifting huge weight and nobody can match your size! Imagine your muscles blowing up to monster proportion as you as you work each body-part. **Many bodybuilders do this and as we know, "What the mind believes the body soon achieves."**

When you are preparing for your workout, imagine yourself turning into any sort of hero that comes to mind. You have a mission to take care of, and nothing in the world will stop you. You are going to destroy that weight, and become the hero that will save the world and take care of business. Sound corny to you? If so, you probably won't be the monster you so aspire to become.

You just have to change. You've had enough workouts that are lackluster and produce doubts in your mind as to whether you were productive or not. Isn't it time to put all that behind you and take it to the next level? It's time to separate yourself from the rest around you, and to start growing as the bodybuilder you could be and should be. There are no more excuses; get real or go home.

This is an extremely important aspect to leaving the beginning bodybuilder level and becoming an intermediate bodybuilder. Until you can stay mentally focused in the gym and lay it all on the line every time you hit the weights you will never make the gains you want. You really want to develop a champion physique and not just be another chump staring at all the different bodies hoping to be tougher than the next guy? **Next time you lift, let nothing stop you, especially not yourself!**

<u>Finding your motivation</u>

This is it folks, the big secret to making a body transformation like I did. It's not some ultimate workout nor is it some radical new diet; **it is simply finding what motivates you to accomplish your goals. To truly commit yourself, you must find something that will give you the drive to push though barriers that normally hold you back.** I know during my transformation there were times that I didn't think I was going make it. I just kept my goals in mind and was constantly finding things to keep me motivated. Without the proper motivation, you will get nothing accomplished. This is a fact.

Getting started

Stages of change model: Use this model as a road map to your success. It is important to know where you are when you are making a big change in your life, especially if you fall off track somewhere. This model worked very well for me in making my transformation a smooth one.

Stages of change:

- **Pre contemplation stage**- You should be through this stage already if you are reading this book with any implications of getting into shape.

- **Contemplation stage**- This is most like the stage you are in now. You are thinking about making a change in your physical appearance.

- **Decision stage**- You will be in this stage when you have made the decision to commit to the challenge you have presented to yourself.

- **Commitment stage**- This is where you are pursuing your goals to make the change. Most people fall short of their goals and get discouraged at this stage. This is why finding something that truly motivates you is important.

- **Maintenance stage**- If you make it this far; congratulations. You have reached your goals. Now you need to maintain what you have done. Don't fall short at this stage. You don't want to undermine what you have worked so hard to accomplish.

Genetic limitations

As I am sure you already know we all come in many different shapes and sizes. Some of us are better suited for some things than others. Some of us are great runners, and some of us would get whooped by my grandmother. Anyway, what I am trying to say is we all have varying body types. Genetic limitations do exist that keep us from looking like those people we see in magazines.

I believe it is important to be straight up with people, and not feed them unrealistic lies to make them feel good. I learned this from a professor in college, who is also a personal trainer. If a potential client came up to him with a picture of Arnold Schwarzenegger or Claudia Schiffer and said, "Make me look like this." He would say, "Sorry, I can't make you look like that. It is genetically impossible." Of course, they would leave in disgust and find another trainer who would feed them an appealing line to get their business.

"Sure, I can make you look just like this." The unscrupulous trainer would say. Well, the funny thing was, after a couple months of no results, the potential client would always come back to my professor and say, "Ok, what can you do for me." With no hostility, he would present them with realistic goals that they could attain.

I hope you understand we are not all meant to be champion bodybuilders, but that doesn't mean we can't be the best that we can be. Never base your results on someone else's results. It's about improving the body that has been given to you that you should base your results on. There are three main body types and there is a way to figure out what kind of body type we most likely have. We all fall into one or a combination of two. Here is a description of the body types so you can figure out which type you most likely are:

- **Ectomorph**- This body type consists of those who have a more slender, lanky builds, and smaller bone structures. They usually have very fast metabolisms, making it hard for them to build muscle. On the other hand, excess body fat is rarely a problem due to their fast metabolisms.

- **Mesomorph**- With a medium sized bone structure and moderate metabolism, body fat and muscle size can be easily manipulated. This is the best body type suited for bodybuilding, because the body can easily lose body fat while gaining muscle.

- **Endomorph**- This body type belongs typically to those who are known as big boned. They have larger bone structures and slower metabolisms. Although very easy for them to gain muscle, body fat is usually a problem.

No matter what body type you have you can always improve what you've been born with. If you have a body type that doesn't appeal to you, don't feel trapped. There is always room for improvement. You will just have to put the work in the gym to get the results you are looking for. You can do it, forget what others say and just believe in yourself.

Motivators such as goals really help

I have made attempts in the past to get into shape, but for one reason or another I would always fall short of my goals. I have learned that the reason I never reached my goals was my approach was wrong. I had failed before ever beginning. Here are some things that I needed in order to truly commit myself.

Short term goals

Start by making a mental or physical list of realistic goals that you can achieve in a short amount of time. For my 12-week transformation, I set monthly goals for my body fat percentage. I think part of my success came from reaching every short-term goal.

Long-term goals, these are goals in which you plan to reach over a longer period of time. You could say "I plan to compete in my first bodybuilding show in one year's time." That could be a realistic long-term goal.

It is important to find what motivates you. What motivates me to stay committed may not interest you at all. Depending on your goals, you should make commitments that work in favor of your goals. For example, if you are looking to shed a couple pounds for summer, you don't want to do a 12-week challenge like I did. You may want to use looking good in your bathing suit as motivation. Just make sure your motivation is strong enough to get you to where your goals are.

Take pictures

Whatever your goal, I believe this is a great place to start. If you are sure or not sure what motivates you, use this method to chart your progress. The camera doesn't lie, and it will tell you what you have improved and what is lacking. Start with a couple pictures of your before self and two months later take some more pictures. If you have been committed, you may be amazed by the results. I know I was! I have many friends and clients using this method to motivate themselves and to chart progress with great success.

Advice

I believe in the words of Bruce Lee when it comes to training and diet: "No way is the right way." This means nothing is perfect. You have to find what works for you. Trial and error is the key. I am not saying for you to try and re-invent the wheel, someone has already done that for you. I am saying there are ways to improve the wheel to fit you better.

Remember, whatever your goals, there must be something that motivates you to get there. If motivation is lost, all is lost. Always know what stage you are in when making any kind of significant change if you plan on making a smooth transition to where you are trying to get. Also, don't ever let genetic limitations hold you back. You can always make improvement no matter what your genetic body type is. With this being said, I hope you all find what it is that keeps the ball rolling in the right direction towards your future goals.

Get motivated

Let's back up for a minute before we review the steps toward goal achievement. What got you into bodybuilding? Was it seeing a bodybuilding show? Was it the incredibly huge and muscular kid next door? Your older brother or sister who bodybuilds? Whatever it was, it no doubt fostered in you a deep, abiding sense of passion for bodybuilding.

That's the way all champions begin, with abiding passion for what they do. With such passion, motivation almost always comes naturally. Passion is a hard word to define. What "turns your crank" may be different from anyone else. It's easier to describe what passion is not:

Passion is not a need to achieve. Instead, it's a burning desire to exceed all bounds! It's not commitment to excellence, but utter disdain for anything less! And, it's not endless hours of practice. It's perfect practice! It's not ability to cope. Rather, it's total domination of all situations! And it's not setting unrealistic or vague goals, because doing so too often prescribes performance limits! Passion is not doing what it takes to win. Instead, it's doing what it takes to exceed! It most certainly is not force of skill or muscle. Rather, it's the explosive, calamitous force of will!

If you believe in and practice these things, then for you, winning is neither everything nor the only thing. It's a foregone conclusion! But if, along the way, you somehow stumble, profit from the experience. Then, vow, by the power of Almighty God, it'll never happen again.

So, you see, passion is all consuming. That is what it takes to become a champion, and that is what it'll take for you to achieve your ultimate bodybuilding goals. If you haven't acquired passion, seek it first. Find it. Do not begin without it, for you will be severely limited in your quest for greatness.

Incentive: The mother of motivation

Motivation and passion begins and ends with incentive. You have to know what you want and why you want it, and achieving it may be reward in and of itself. This is called "intrinsic" reward. "Extrinsic" rewards are such things as money, trophies or prizes. In both cases, the rewards serve as incentive to continue.

In bodybuilding, this may mean that achieving a specific improvement provides the incentive for going after it. More strength, stamina, cuts or sheer muscle mass are various incentives. But they may also be a part of larger incentives such as being liked and admired, being a winner or achiever, enjoying success, shaping a personal identity, gaining peer acceptance, and so on. Recognize incentive as a powerful motivating force, not as something potentially destructive, evil, trivial or shameful.

Steps to goal attainment

1. Set realistic short-term goals.

2. Short-term goals should lead you to a long-term goal. Allow for occasional setbacks along the way, but regard them as learning experiences, thereby turning those setbacks into something positive.

3. Set a training schedule and stick to it.

4. Make pain and fatigue work for you, as signs that your all-out effort is helping you attain your goals.

5. Constantly challenge yourself in your training.

6. Devise your own, personal definition of success. It's what you say it is, not what someone else says.

7. Believe in yourself and foster positive aggression in your training.

8. Build a strong ego, but a restrained one.

Your emotional state

Your mind and your emotions are tightly tied together. It's up to you to find a balance between them and exert absolute control over them. Your emotional state plays a large role in your overall training. The way you're feeling inside has repercussions for your behavior and performance on the outside. There are many different factors, which go into the makeup of a solid emotional base. Some of these factors are:

- **Personal life**

- **Sexual life**

- **Family life**

- **Job**

- **Daily schedule**

- **Diet**

- **Financial matters**

- **Health concerns, and, most importantly**

- **Self-esteem**

Your own self-esteem contributes greatly to the level of your sports performance. Self-esteem can vary greatly within the time confines of a single training session, and it can mean the difference between winning and losing in a competition setting. One minute you may hate yourself over an error you've committed on the posing platform or in the gym, and a few moments later you could reverse that feeling completely by performing exceptionally.

This sort of event can, and often does, lead to superlative performance throughout the remainder of your training session in the gym, or in your onstage performance. In either case, your mental appraisal of yourself, your self-esteem, counts for a great deal in your performance.

The Doctor Says:
As far as self-esteem goes, what you think about yourself is always more important than what anyone else thinks of you.

However common this sort of scenario may be, it is not the sort of thing to be sought after. It would be far better if your self-esteem going into the gym or competition were such that only superlative performance throughout was possible. Day after day, month after month, building only the possibility of success into your training by careful, integrated application of science will tend to maintain peak mental attitude and feelings of self-esteem. Success begets success.

Fear of failure

Fear, depression, anxiety or over-arousal can all lead to sub-par training or competition performance. For every winner, there are many losers, and often the distinguishing feature between the two is attitude, positive thinking and the absence of inhibiting fear.

Fear of the competition, for instance, can put you in a defeatist frame of mind even before the competition begins. If you're so "psyched out" that you consider your opponent unbeatable, then you have defeated yourself. Instead, your goal is to foster belief in yourself, train hard to achieve the means to victory, and then realize you have made your belief work for you.

All your success comes first out of belief in yourself. In fact, belief and success go hand in hand. Once you rid yourself of fear, you begin to see yourself as potentially better than your opponent, and that's the key to winning! In a state of fear, you will never see yourself as potentially better than your opponent. So, it's obvious then, that **your state of mind determines, to a large extent, whether or not you ever "see" victory.**

Fear of injury

Fear of injury is another inhibiting factor. Doubtless you've heard of the "oft-injured" athlete who is forever on the disabled list. Sometimes, when this athlete returns to active play, he/she tends to be slightly gun-shy, afraid of injury, and might even alter his/her style of play to protect from injury. **Ironically, playing to protect yourself against injury often leads to it, because you're pulling up, not following through with movements and contracting your muscles irregularly.**

The same sort of protective training occurs in bodybuilding. The effects of a torn rotator cuff, a pulled hamstring or whatever injury you may have suffered all tend to linger long after the injury is healed sufficiently to be trained again. Being careful is prudent. But being unreasonably careful will serve naught but keeping you from your goal.

Fear of success

Picture this scenario. Your best buddy is your training partner. He means a lot to you, and you don't want to embarrass him by showing him up with your superior physique, strength or pain tolerance. Where does this lead? Believe me; this sort of "fear" is not all that uncommon! Being pals is one thing. But a real pal will recognize your superior abilities. Turn your friendship with your training partner into a healthy, constructive, friendly competitive situation!

If you feel that your training partner is holding you back, don't train with him anymore! If you're an aspiring elite bodybuilder, your training program isn't going to match his anyway. Being buddy-buddy to the extent of following the identical training programs rep-per-rep, exercise-per-exercise, day after day is downright stupid.

Other situations involving fear of success:

1. Not wishing to attain your ultimate goal for fear of no longer having anything to strive for;

2. Not wishing to be forced to accept the socio-psychological responsibilities associated with being the champion, and

3. Not wanting to totally commit to doing everything necessary in order to become the champion. The first step in eliminating these sorts of fears is to realize that they exist. Then, it's a simple matter of intellectually reasoning as to why such fears exist and how utterly silly such fears really are. A skilled sports hypnotherapist or sports psychologist may be able to assist you in eliminating these potentially debilitating roadblocks to success.

Discipline

Discipline is what people say that I have, but it not like you're born with it. I wasn't born with this as well. Discipline comes from a need. What that means is that you have to have the need to be the best or the need to be the strongest like myself.

What is discipline?

Discipline is the willingness to sacrifice things to achieve your goal. Bodybuilders do this when they diet. They sacrifice hangout time with the buddies to focus on training and resting for their next contest. Power lifters also do this as well when it gets close to a meet; they have to be focused mentally and physically to make sure they are on track. But those are for guys who compete; what about the guys who don't who have everything available except discipline. What do you do?

The Doctor Says:
I need to make it clear that discipline doesn't mean that you deprive yourself or torture yourself. All of life's choices have consequences, good and bad. You just have to choose which consequences you want.

First you have to ask yourself: do you want it? It all goes back to desire. Do you have that burning desire for what you do? If you do, then you're willing to make sacrifices. And when I mean sacrifices, I do mean that. You have to be willing to sacrifice going out to the club and drinking, hanging out with friends, sleeping in, etc. to make your goal.

I remember getting up at 5:00am to train three days a week it was simply because I was willing and able to do that. This meant I had to sacrifice staying up late when I want to. You have to be willing to be able to come into the gym at the same time every training day.

Training with discipline

Discipline also comes into play during your training. You have to be willing to do your best on the exercises you do and that you have to be willing to do even the hardest one including squats and deadlifts and the alike. This will test your discipline to the max.

For instance, Lifter X tells his friends that he wants to bench 400lbs. by the end of winter. His friends want to see this so they set a day and Lifter X begins training, but is lacking in discipline.

What does he do? He first starts off by getting on the Internet and getting any and all information on increasing his bench so that he can be prepared the right way and to setup his workouts. He then decides to take supplements to help, like protein and creatine. He changes his eating habits by taking out junk foods and having one cheat day.

Lifter X also restricts his going out to the clubs to once a month up until the last two months of training. Where he will be thinking nothing else than to bench 400lbs. and he puts himself on a daily schedule which will require him to go to the gym before he quits for the day and whenever he's not training or working, he'll be resting.

Now from what I've given you, do you think that Lifter X can stick with the program? I would think so. He decided that by having a goal, he can put his energy into increasing his bench press and by being driven and disciplined he thinks that he can do it! So what happens? Lifter X does the 400lbs. bench, but now he wants to keep increasing it and now is willing to do anything and everything to be the best at it.

Concentration

Success in sports performance can be likened to the practice of Zen masters. The concentration is so complete; there is no consciousness of concentration. The player must be one with his sport in order to execute it to his/her optimal ability.

You have no doubt been in a situation where your entire attention was so rapt and absorbed in one thought that you completely blocked out all others. This was probably due to your high concentration level on some thought of great importance to you. This kind of focus can be a confidence builder.

The more you focus on what you're working to achieve, the less distractions enter your awareness. This lifts you out of the state of mind that can't "see" success. **Once you begin to "see" success, you consider yourself potentially better than the competition.** Little by little, you concentrate more and more, until you're unaware of anything in your way. You see your way clearly to victory and success. This is total concentration.

This kind of total concentration comes to those who develop total self-confidence. You must have high self-esteem, high motivation, and be consistent in your training program. You must develop your mind to the point that total concentration is merely a learned response, one you never consciously think about anymore.

Then, apply this sort of laser focus rep-per-rep and set-per-set in your workouts. Apply it in following your daily-integrated training program. **Just as success begets success, imperfect practice makes your performance imperfect.**

Be an example

Be an example. If you're not competing, tell your friends and/or family that you're shooting for particular goal like getting ripped for the summer, having a big bench before football season, gaining 20lbs before spring, or whatever you want your goal to be. But it's not like signing a contract, once you say that you're going to get bigger, you have to commit to it and having them on you about it will make you that much more disciplined. **Trust me, discipline is easier to get than most people think.** It's the things that you have to sacrifice in order to get what you want.

6 keys to successful bodybuilding

To make clear the simplicity of bodybuilding I've arranged a list of six basic keys to successful training. They're nothing new and read like the same stuff in any motivational book on the market today. Yet they offer valuable insight and are essential to getting started and sticking to it.

1. Set a realistic goal - short and long term.

2. Plan an orderly and thorough routine to train the entire body.

3. Make a commitment to stick to your routine for 4-5 weeks - - to begin to see changes and benefits, develop perseverance and create a habit.

4. Enthusiasm for training must be recognized as the main and driving force to perform successfully.

5. Ease into a training program with a wholesome, thoughtful nutritional plan - proper food, order and amount of consumption.

6. Be confident from the beginning that the application of these sound principles will produce the desired results.

GOAL SETTING

Be realistic in your goal setting. It's important from the very beginning and throughout your training to experience victory in each and every workout. Ease into your training with good energy, being careful not to overload yourself and fall victim to mental and physical burnout. Planning to look like Rambo by the end of summer will be frustrating and you may give up your training entirely.

ORDER IN TRAINING

Decide how much time you have to devote to your training - how many hours per day and how many days per week. Based on this schedule, design an orderly and efficient routine that includes only basic exercises. Working your mid-section first, followed by chest, back shoulders, biceps, triceps and legs is always a good rule of thumb. Choose two exercises per bodypart, three to four sets of 8 to 12 reps with a day's rest between muscle groups if you're just getting started.

In organizing an exercise program, keep your eyes and ears open. Scan the Web, magazines and books, visit the gyms and get input from your friends and mentors. An orderly and intelligent training routine is the major tool in achieving your bodybuilding goals.

COMMITMENT

We now come to commitment, the Big Power Switch of our mental mechanism to see if we have the juice to crank over the engine and keep it running. Commitment is your personal promise - your word of honor - to realize your challenge and is vital in aspiration. The naturally occurring ingredients of commitment are consistency, persistence and determination. These gut disciplines engaged with patience and faith set you in positive motion toward your muscular goals.

ENTHUSIASM

Each workout is a unique and separate experience unto itself. Events of the day, mood, energy levels and tensions effect every performance differently. Gather up as much enthusiasm as possible before each workout so you enter the gym with energy and a positive attitude. Your training must not become drudgery or a chore that has to be done. This is negative energy, producing negative results and must be willfully resisted.

PACE AND ATTITUDE

Keep your workouts tight and efficient, leaving no room for boredom or idle thought. You should quickly develop a mature training attitude allowing no interruptions in the flow of exercise from start to finish. This is not to suggest that you hurry in your training. A hurried attitude produces anxiety, nervousness and agitation, resulting in negative performance and loss of concentration. Quite the opposite, here I encourage a steady lean on your training - setting a vigorous pace that reflects excitement, confidence and determination.

Become totally involved with each workout, each set and each rep. Focus on the performance of the exercise, the muscles involved and the feelings that result. Look for your particular groove and sense the burn. Training form is your priority and practice makes perfect. Learn to lift weights smoothly, sacrificing the poundage used to gain quality in your performance. Don't be anxious to overload your body and struggle to lift more than you can handle. This will create poor style and result in disappointment. These register as failures and drain your resources.

Once the basic foundation has settled, good work habits have developed and your groove has been established, you're on your way and ready to grow.

<u>Composing a vision</u>

When composing your vision I encourage you to brainstorm and randomly jot down any ideas, thoughts, dreams, and/or goals that come to mind. Dare to dream, dreaming of everything that motivates you to strive towards your goals on a consistent basis. Including the following may assist you in developing an awesome vision.

1) **Listing out all of the reasons why you are seriously committed to reaching your goals.** Most choose to do what they do to get a certain feeling. I ask you, why are you motivated to chase your dreams and goals? Is it because you want to do something that is meaningful to you? Do you want to make an impact on others through your life? Will achieving your goals give you pride and honor towards yourself? Do you have something to prove?

Whatever your reasons are, take time to sit down and list the most important reasons that have significant meaning to you. These very reasons will keep you motivated throughout the year.

2) **List the major steps and actions that you must complete to get to your ultimate destination.** On your journey, there will be certain key steps and actions that you will have to take. When creating your vision it is important to recognize a few of these actions and steps.

3) **Recognize your ultimate purpose for working hard now and in the future.** You cannot hit a target without having a bull's-eye to aim for.

10 benefits of reviewing your vision daily

1. You are forced to create a plan when creating a vision

How many individuals do you know that have really taken time out to decide what it is that they wish to attain from their efforts? Visions serve as guides to destinations. By investing a little time and creating a vision you will place yourself way ahead of others in your field. Creating a vision forces you to determine what you want to accomplish, where you want to be, and who you want to become. The visions that I have created over the past year have had a massive impact on who I am becoming and where I am today.

2. You will work in a more direct manner

How much human resources such as time and energy have you spent working towards something? Notice that I said "something" and did not state a specific goal, when you have a vision and you review it daily, you are working in a focused manner. This will allow you to stop zigzagging and keeps you focused. Additionally, your vision reminds why you are committed to achieving what is so important to you throughout the year.

3. Visions allow you to make the right decisions, daily

Once you have a vision you will find yourself making the "right choices". Intelligent, meaningful, goal oriented, focused, and purpose-driven decisions will be made unconsciously. These things will begin to come automatically because your subconscious mind is suddenly aware of the implications that they will have on your future. **Reviewing your vision daily, plants the concept in your subconscious mind, therefore you tend to work toward your goals without being consciously aware.** Having a vision will assist you in staying away from ineffective, time-consuming methods that distract you and tend to run you off course.

4. You become accountable for your actions

If you were to be reminded daily of how bad doing the things that will negatively affect are to reaching your goals how long do you think it would take to get you thinking straight again? **Reading your vision everyday makes you become accountable for all of your actions.** You do not forget about the promises that you have made to yourself. You constantly follow through with the actions, steps, motivation, intelligent decisions, and daily tasks.

5. The challenging times that you have will become easier

Ever heard of the expressions "I am on an uphill battle, I take one step forward and two steps back, and I am fighting a losing battle"? These expressions are used when describing an endeavor that people have found to be extremely difficult. Do you feel this way sometimes in your bodybuilding journey? I personally know the familiar feeling having felt this way several times through my bodybuilding career! However, **having a vision gave me confidence to stick with my theories and beliefs even when times were tough.** A vision gives you the ability to hang in there even when it seems like the only one who believes in your capabilities, goals, and dreams are none other that yourself.

Believing in and consistently reviewing your vision gives you a unique ability, which draws you toward accomplishing your goals instead of toward the everlasting uphill battle. **Your vision makes your journey much more positive.** People, in general, do not have a problem striving when things are going in the right direction, however, good times do not last forever. During every journey, or when you are pursuing anything that is worth having/accomplishing you will encounter the toughest of challenges. These challenges are known as the obstacles of life itself.

Setbacks can be injuries, feeling hopeless thinking that you have tried everything when trying to improve a certain body part or having influential-special people leave you because they do not fully support or understand your passion for the sport of bodybuilding. These setbacks can be devastating and may threaten your willing strive for excellence, but visions help you adjust to these setbacks and disappointing events. **Creating your vision, believing in it, and reviewing it daily gives you the power to continue climbing to the summit of your destination.**

6. Visions make you find ways to meet your goals

The individuals that try "just once more" are the people who eventually reach ultimate success. Creating and reviewing a vision everyday unleashes the genius inside. You suddenly find ways and have great ideas that assist you in reaching your goals. These ways make it possible to continue to work toward your ultimate goals day in and day out. No more excuses!

7. You find ways to overcome difficult challenges

Persistence is needed in order to reach your goals. The creative genius in us all comes alive when we review our vision daily and you will find solutions to inevitable problems and challenges, which occur along the way.

8. People become valuable assets to you

Being in the right company this year will assist you in getting every ounce of opportunity out of this year. A vision allows you to effectively utilize people in your very life to assist you in achieving your dreams. You instinctively know who must be removed or avoided from your life never allowing them to steer you wrong.

9. Visions allow you to realize what you have accomplished

Reviewing your vision will allow you to realize that you are steadily making progress and will someday reach your goals. Realizing what you have already accomplished through reading your vision will "pump you up" when you have failed to recognize how much you have already accomplished. Most people fail to appreciate the victories that they experience. Creating a vision and realizing that we will not just wake up one day and be where we want to be, you will learn to appreciate what you have or are achieving along the way to your ultimate goal.

10. You will enjoy striving for your goals

Creating a vision and reviewing it daily saves time, allows you to work in a concise manner, make the right decisions, find solutions to any obstacle, remain optimistic, enlist help from others, and appreciate your accomplishments through your journey. Having a vision and following this method leaves little to no doubt that you will enjoy the journey. This is what having and reviewing a vision will do for you so sit down focus and create your vision.

Goal setting 101

When this year comes to an end, what will you have accomplished? What results have stemmed from all of your hard efforts? People have great potential. Human beings are the most remarkable and intelligent life form known to mankind. Sadly, what we as humans actually accomplish is rather disappointing. What you have achieved up to this point in time is not a result of what you can do, it is not a result of your potential, and it is actually a result of what you have done. What we must understand is that our level of success lies in what we actually get ourselves to do. What we actually act upon, believe in, and are passionate about. What we are willing to follow through with battling the struggles associated with the challenge in order to reach our goals.

Dreams, goals, and potential are useless without having the ability to follow through with them. We must continue to follow through, always stepping closer to our goals. Furthermore, we must do this consistently if we plan on achieving our dreams, goals, and utilizing our potential to the max.

Doctor's Prescription:
This all comes down to taking action. Most people think but never do. I can't say this enough: Take action, take action, take action!

If we could clearly see the rewards which are awaiting our hard work, perseverance, and consistency we would have an easier time staying motivated to follow through with our plan. Do you have a plan, or is your goal merely a dream? Planning is a must in order for success to occur. Actions, steps, motivation, intelligent decisions, and daily tasks are a necessity when planning to accomplish what we want most out of our lives. For most of us it will be bodybuilding and fitness related.

Charles Dickens's "A Christmas Story", the character Scrooge had the opportunity to travel through time allowing him to take a look into his future. This allowed him to see how his personal actions, steps, motivation, decisions, and daily tasks that he had taken over the years had shaped the outcome of his life. Scrooge had to be scared into changing his life for the better; he was able to see the horrid direction that he was heading for. Scrooge also changed because he saw how great life would be when he did the right things. The point of this story, Scrooge's guide, who was the ghost of Christmas future, showed Scrooge how great life would turn out to be if he only changed and began to follow through on the good actions, steps, intelligent decisions, and daily tasks thus creating a happy life for all.

Do you not wish that you too could get a sneak peek into the future allowing you to see first-hand what is going to happen in the future? Ever wonder if your efforts toward bodybuilding, fitness, training, sleeping, cardio, and eating are going to payoff rewarding you with your bodybuilding related goals? Do you ever wonder if you will ever achieve your ultimate goals? How awesome would it be to know all of this in advance? Would life not be easier during really challenging times if you knew that you would meet all of your goals?

It would be really comforting for you to know that you were going to finally use the right strategies. These strategies would allow you to build the ultimate physique, the same physique that you have desired for as long as you can remember. You would now have peace of mind, pride, confidence, and certainty in your corner. You would be 100% sure that all would work out fine. You would not even care that it would take you the entire year. You would be more than willing to try over 100 new techniques on your journey to making your goals come true.

Well, let us not forget that we still have an imagination. Let us imagine that the ghost of Christmas future took us into the future. Not only did we take that amazing trip, we saw what we wanted to see (us meeting our goals). Now, knowing that you were going to reach your goals, how differently will you act? What will you do, will you be more patient knowing that you will be rewarded at the end of the year? Will you be more persistent knowing that hard work does payoff? Would anything be able to distract you and stand in your way of success? Do you ever think that you will miss another workout or cheat on your diet when you have made a promise to yourself that you would not let this happen?

If you were able to get a preview of how your life would flow in the future would you be more of a risk taker? Do you not think that you would have more courage and confidence? Would you not enjoy and cherish the bodybuilding journey much more? **Creating this optimistic vision of the future will make the journey easier.** Although it may be a fantasy, having an opportunity to see the future would be great. So let's go for it, use your mind to invent the bodybuilding journey, which you are working towards experiencing this year. To do so you must create your very own personal vision.

A vision is sort of like a mission statement. The vision, which you should create, is a mental image of what you are working on now. Your personal vision will constantly remind you of how you should or want to act on a consistent basis, day in and day out. Your vision should include the things that not only want to but also now see yourself accomplishing them (remember we took that trip with the ghost of the future). You can be brave and extend your vision including things that you are working toward accomplishing beyond next year.

Make your vision short and concise. Written out, it should be a compilation of statements, encouraging words, phrases, and reminders. You should constantly review these to assist you in staying on the right track. **Limit your vision to 4-5 paragraphs consisting of goals, standards, daily actions, daily goals, and inspirational quotes.** This will remind you to do these things in order to become who you ultimately want to be and accomplish. Review this vision twice daily to stay on track and focused.

Bodybuilding goal checklist

Desire - Desire is the force that drives you towards your bodybuilding goals. It is what motivates you to endure those intense, physical workouts. You have to want your goal badly. If you don't want it, believe me, nobody else wants it for you!

Belief - You must believe, without a doubt, that you can achieve your bodybuilding goals. Belief is the foundation of success.

Write it down - Your goals need to be written, or they are merely wishes. If a goal is worth setting, then it is worth writing. Write it in as much detail as possible.

Determine the benefits - Why do you want this goal so badly? If you cannot think of a good enough reason, is it worth going after? Make a list of all the benefits you will receive from achieving your goal.

Analyze your current status - Where are you currently in your bodybuilding endeavor? Until you know where you are now, you will never know where you need to be. The most detailed map in the world is useless if you do not know your current location.

Set a deadline - When do you want to achieve your goal? On most goals, you need a deadline, or you will not strive to achieve it in a timely manner. Deadlines create a sense of urgency.

Identify obstacles - Be prepared to face hurdles along the way. But if you are prepared to handle the worse, everything else that comes your way is a walk in the park.

Identify the knowledge you will need - We often must learn new things to completely accomplish our goals. Whether it is a new program or a textbook you are reading, identify the knowledge you will need to know in order to reach your goals.

Identify people to assist you - We often need others to help us get what we want. And we should reciprocate the process; help others get what they need and want. Don't be ashamed to admit you need help achieving your goal. Surround yourself with people that have a positive impact on your life. Get rid of those who don't.

Devise a plan - Put down, on paper, and in detail, how you are going to achieve your goal. Put down the activities you will need to get involved in so that you reach your goal. Most people do not have a fitness plan devised; they just wander from machine to machine, exercise to exercise. Develop a plan to get to where you want to be.

Create a mental image - Imagine your goal already attained. Create a crystal clear picture of you enjoying your goal. The more you think about enjoying your goal, the more your subconscious begins to work and move you closer to the attainment of your goal.

Resolve never to give up - Finally, resolve to never, ever quit. You must determine the price you have to pay to achieve your fitness goals, and then resolve to pay that price. Be persistent and determined to reach that finish line. You will be a much stronger person for it in the end.

The more of these items you can include in your routine, the closer you will be to success in your bodybuilding endeavors.

Making dreams a reality and setting goals

We all aspire to achieve something very important to us through training. It may be improving the way we look, our health, or help our sporting performance. The problem is so few of us actually achieve what we are striving for from our work. The question then becomes why? The number one reason I hear from people is they "lack motivation." Of course, if you don't view what you are doing as a priority, your chances for success are very low. However, motivation is different for every person. The key is to find what gets each individual excited. I am going to outline some tips to finding what ideas keep one excited about training so that everyone gives himself or herself the best opportunity to succeed.

10 steps to setting and attaining goals

1. Understand what flicks your switch & what pulls the plug

In the context of weight training, sports psychologists refer to this self-evaluation process as understanding your motivational style. In other words, you need to figure out what motivates you and what de-motivates you. The former is usually pretty obvious; the latter is often what causes you to toss your gym bag in the closet and leave it there to rot. I've encountered people who've made up their minds to lose 10 pounds of body fat, only to give up the moment someone tells them they'll never succeed. That initial motivation was so weak that a single comment was enough to upend it. Other people are perfectionists who'd rather be sedentary than active, feeling that if they exercise, they might fall short of what for them is the "perfect" body. Then you have the underachievers, who set their goals low even though the sky may be the limit. Understanding what motivates you is the first step in sticking with your program.

2. Set goals

Once you analyze your motivational style, you can begin doing the things that will make it work for you. For example, you can now set appropriate goals and list the steps you must take to achieve them. Setting long-term goals, such as how you want to look a year from now, will make it easier for you to determine the constituent shorter-term goals, whether measured by months, weeks or even individual workouts.

3. Get with the (right) program

Once you set your goals, you need to tailor your training to achieve them. I once counseled a woman who was frustrated with her exercise program. She wanted to "tone up," but after four months, she hadn't seen any results. When I asked her to outline her regimen, she explained that she was doing anaerobic interval-type running three times a week. Wrong program! Her goal was to look better in her swimsuit, so her program should have combined weight training and aerobic exercise with proper nutrition. Inappropriate programs lead to noncompliance. If you need a trainer's help to design a suitable program, by all means hire one. As an added benefit, you'll be accountable to someone else for your continued success.

4. Tell a friend

Make a list of the most significant people in your life — those individuals whose opinions you desire, value and respect. Rely on these people to help you stay focused on your exercise program. Something as simple as a few words of encouragement, or companionship during your workout, can really help. And to the extent that these significant others understand your exercise regimen and nutritional strategies, they can become far more effective supporters. Who knows — maybe they'll follow your lead and start training themselves.

5. Visualize

Visualization gives you the power to use thoughts, images and feelings to create your own reality. By envisioning your desired body shape, you increase the possibility of realizing that image. Visualization allows you to pursue your fitness potential by creating a mental picture of whom and what you can become, which increases motivation.

6. Become a student

Elite athletes live and breathe their sport. You may not need to reproduce that same level of dedication, but those individuals can still teach you a valuable lesson. Read as much as you can about weight training, bodybuilding, aerobic exercise and nutrition. Attend fitness seminars and clinics hosted by exercise specialists. Knowledge enhances motivation, which leads to a deeper commitment.

7. Connect your mind & body

Your nervous system has an amazing, sophisticated relationship with the rest of your body. Any time you move, your brain is inundated with thousands of signals. It then makes decisions and sends signals back through the nervous system, where they're broken down into simpler, more precise messages intended for each muscle fiber. That helps explain the mind-muscle connection to which so many champion bodybuilders allude. To improve your workouts, learn to listen to what your body is telling your brain, and vice versa. When you become more aware of this mind-body connection, you'll be better prepared for the workout to follow.

8. Reward yourself

You work hard in the gym, busting your tail after you've already invested yourself in work or school. Why not bribe — er, reward — yourself with a gift for sticking with the program? I recommend that all beginners reward themselves at least once a month, regardless of results. Setting a Herculean goal (for example, losing 25 pounds) that you must reach before you reward yourself misses the point. By sticking with your training, you're making exercise part of your regular lifestyle. The weight loss will eventually take care of itself.

9. Define success on your own terms

Just because someone you know defines success as bench-pressing 350 pounds or building 20-inch arms doesn't mean you should, too. Define success for yourself and be prepared to celebrate once you achieve it. People who take time to savor small achievements en route to greater success are usually more motivated to continue with their weight training than people who are never satisfied.

10. Go slow, go steady

Bodybuilding isn't about overnight success or automatic changes — it's about making a commitment to a healthy lifestyle that includes exercise and sound nutrition. Don't look at the professional bodybuilders in this magazine and become disillusioned when you don't look like them after six months of training. Most elite bodybuilders have been committed to the bodybuilding lifestyle for many years. Having great genetics is merely a bonus for them. Stay the course and you'll see significant changes in the shape of your body. Keep a logbook of your workouts and body measurements and, over time, you won't even need a mirror to see the improvements your training and diet have wrought. They'll be staring back from the page in black and white.

Define a specific goal

This may seem so elementary, but many people that have emailed me rarely have the makings of a well thought-out goal. Spending time to write out your goals and learning what makes the foundation of goal setting is so important because this will serve as your base of motivation. The vaguer you are the more this will set you up for failure because you will be training without a purpose. So, here are some principles of goal setting:

1. Measurable: Bodybuilding is a tough sport because it is so subjective. The more subjective a goal the more frustrating it can be because setting a standard of measurement is so difficult. Being able to see progress is what is going to keep so many of us going. Having definitive numbers can provide us with such information. People either want to lose body fat, gain muscle, or the combination of the two.

However, the problem arises when trainers have no idea of their starting point and where they want to end. If you do not have this information then how are you going to tell if you are moving towards achieving your goal? Right now, sit down and write out one physical goal for yourself that can be measured.

2. Optimal level of difficulty: A goal cannot be too hard or too easy. Without the sense of a challenge one will not push themselves and strive for greater levels. At the same time, if the goal is too difficult then failure in inevitable. The key is to define a goal that will challenge you and be reasonable to achieve.

3. Meaningful: This is my favorite principle. Why do you want to achieve this physical goal? Don't just say because you want to look good. Instead write three ways in which it will improve your life. The more meaning your goal has in your overall life the more of a priority it becomes in your mind. Most people want to change their bodies for a variety of reasons. Improving self-confidence in the work place so that you are more successful in your career, feeling more attractive so you can be more comfortable in social circumstances, or become better at your sport because you want to achieve a college scholarship are just a few examples. The more meaning you can create for you goal the more valuable the goal becomes. Right now write down three ways achieving your goal will improve your life.

4. Must fit personal value systems: All of us have values that hopefully dictate much of our actions. These values help us decide what is important to us and what we base our decisions from. If the goal you have set up does not reflect the values in your life then it can become an unnecessary stress. There is a famous saying, "stress occurs when behaviors do not reflect values." For example, you may want to add 15 pounds of muscle, but you decide to use drugs to accomplish this goal. However, you do not believe in drug use for non-medical purposes. Automatically you are creating conflict between what you value and what you are trying to accomplish. This can cause people to feel very negative about their chosen activity and the once positive goal now instills upsetting feelings.

5. Completion Date: You must have a deadline for your goal. Training can be compared to many aspects of business. Every business that has projects creates a task map, which is considered essential. This map not only outlines what needs to be completed so that the project is successful, but also dates in which not only the overall project is due, but also all the smaller tasks. Setting a date is a way of knowing if your goal is realistic and what you need to perform to finish the goal. This method also allows you to see if you are having difficulty along the way and set up solutions for these problems. Training for a date also provides a level of challenge and a competitive spirit. You have an end in mind which in vital to any project.

6. Willingness to make sacrifices: Listen, any goal is going to require sacrifices. The key is to determine if those sacrifices are reasonable and will result in a greater good. In my earlier days I had tried training people that wanted to make changes, but were not willing to make sacrifices. Without question none of those individuals even came close to their goals. So many people are concerned about not fitting into our societies' norms.

However, if you are trying to achieve something exceptional then you are not going to be normal, as normal is for those that are happy being very average. Sit down and list out the sacrifices that would have to be made to achieve the goal you have set out for yourself. Make sure that those sacrifices do not conflict with your values, beliefs, and are realistic to your situation.

Goal setting conclusion

Many people want me to look at their programs and tell them what they are doing wrong. I always believe in starting with the most obvious and going from there. In most cases the most obvious is the lack of applying the above principles to form a solid foundation for success. So, if you have never heard or implemented the above principles, sit down right now. Get yourself away from distractions and go through each principle and have a goal set based upon the above information, and write it down! I guarantee you will be providing yourself a better opportunity to succeed.

<u>**Blueprint your success**</u>

Do you disappear from the gym into oblivion for weeks on end? Do you hit the snooze button in favor of your morning run? Do you find yourself having a cheat meal every day? I think not. But if you are, don't fret just yet. Whether you aspire to be a muscle-bound freak or a lean-mean-ripped-machine, it takes dedication to see the fruits of your labor. You don't go from dud to stud in the blink of an eye. You need a plan! Try the following and you'll be on track to a killer body faster than you ever imagined.

Go slow at first

Failing to plan is planning to fail. If you want to get big, don't just say, "Whatever it takes, I'll be huge by summer!" Thinking like this may leave you doomed to failure. Picture the task as a pie. Next, cut it up into little pieces and tackle one chunk at a time. For example, over the next 4 weeks, concentrate on gaining 2 pounds, then 5, then 10. Increase your meal frequency from 4 to 5 meals a day, then 6.

Bump up your carbohydrate intake slowly from 1g per pound of bodyweight, to 2 and then to 3, you get my point. This is where a training journal comes in handy. It maps out your quest for a better physique by recording changes in your training, diet, sets, reps etc.

Write it down, write it down, write it down

Find a small notebook to jot down notes on. You can record meals, sets, reps, bodyweight, fat, and even measurements. Nothing feels better than going through your past entries and seeing how far you've come. Everybody is different, and customizing a plan that works for you involves trial and error.

Training logs make the process much easier. Did you hit the pectorals better on an incline bench? Did you get enough sleep each night last week? These things make the difference between a good and great physique. Review your notes once a week and make the appropriate changes to your routine. Just don't be overly meticulous or it'll become tedious and boring.

Small goals = big gains

Instead one big goal i.e. "Get big or die", write down several smaller goals on a sheet of paper and call it your "To do list". For example:

By end of month:

1) 5lbs gain in lean body mass

2) Increase bench press 1 rep max from 225 - 245

3) Add 1 inch to chest and arm measurements

4) Consume 6 meals a day

5) 1.25g of protein per pound of bodyweight.

Note: Plan accordingly for subsequent months.

Small goals are easier to reach than giant, seemingly unattainable ones. They act as milestones you must surpass in order to succeed in your mission. It's like using stepping-stones to cross a river. Slowly but surely you'll get to the other side. **Finally, small accomplishments boost your self-confidence and belief in your ability to succeed.** Remember folks; Chris Cormier's back wasn't built in a day!

Visualize and be positive

No, this isn't some Eastern meditation practice. It's simply a matter of incorporating the power of the mind into the bodybuilding equation. Visualization involves forming mental images and using them to improve your focus and concentration. In addition, it can be applied to almost every facet of bodybuilding; contest, diet, training, recovery etc. For example, if you're preparing for a contest, visualizing yourself on stage in peak condition can keep you motivated to stick with your diet, even through the tough times.

If you tend to wander aimlessly from exercise to exercise at the gym, try the following method. The next time you train, take 5 minutes before to sit in a quiet place and actually think through your routine. Picture yourself performing every exercise and set. Imagine busting every rep out with balls-to-the-wall intensity. The cold, hard iron invigorates your senses as you punish your muscles with heavy weights and strict form. Now, you're focused. Get in, train hard, get out, and watch those muscles grow.

Don't shortchange yourself by thinking you're not going to succeed. If you enter a contest, why not try to win it? I'm not advocating unrealistic thinking. After all, not everyone has the genetics to be the next Jay Cutler. But if you enter into a state of negativity; "I'm never going to get big" / "I'm never going to be strong" then chances are, you never will. **In whatever your pursuit, believe in yourself and your abilities.**

Establish a time frame

Discipline yourself to accomplish certain goals within a time frame. By doing this, you keep yourself accountable and are less likely to slack off. But make sure you're not selling yourself short on time. You're probably not going to pack on 30 pounds on muscle in 4 weeks! One of the biggest mistakes I see bodybuilders make is not giving themselves enough time to reach their goals. They end up over trained, frustrated, and burned out. If you want to lose fat, for example, set a feasible target to lose 4 pounds of fat this month. That equates to one pound of fat a week, which is very doable. So just do it!

Get a training partner

Working out together is a great way to develop a friendship or enrich an existing one. It's always fun to see couples working out together. Better yet, gym buddies gathered around a squat rack giving shouts of "Fight it!" and "Stay tight!" to some dude who's just loaded 405lbs on his back. **Bodybuilding with friends is a great way to stay motivated, just be sure to keep the chitchat to a minimum unless you enjoy unproductive 3-hour workouts.**

Good training partners are precious commodities. They can provide feedback on your form, intensity, overall development etc. If you're less experienced then they are going to them for advice will take a lot of guesswork out of your program. Try setting similar goals and see who reaches them first. A little competition never hurts, right? A training partner can drive you to work harder so that his / her physique doesn't outshine yours. But remember, push yourself to the limits, not over, or you'll get hurt.

Reward yourself

Rewards provide a sense of accomplishment, which in turn encourage you to keep up the good work. Chances are your gym buddies aren't going give you a dime every time you bench 275. Here's your solution. **Once you attain certain goals, go ahead and reward yourself, you deserve it!** They can come in the form of new supplements, bodybuilding magazines, gym apparel, a rare cheat meal, music CDs etc. They don't have to be expensive. Whatever you deem a suitable prize, it shall be. Rewards can turn your intensity up a notch in eager anticipation of the satisfaction to come. In addition, they also help take your mind off a tough week of dieting or after a brutal training session.

Doctor's Prescription:
Reward yourself in all areas of your life. The rewards are the reason you perform a specific task right? Rewards give you something to shoot for.

Blueprint conclusion

If you don't have a blueprint for success, you're not going anywhere. All the "Flex Wheeler" caps and protein powder in the world won't make you big and cut. Instead, a great physique begins in the mind, and can only be achieved through vigilant planning. Dorian Yates started out skinny, but went on to add slabs of rock-hard muscle. He won six Mr. Olympia titles and forged a legacy for himself. True bodybuilders don't start out huge. They don't wake up one morning as genetic freaks. They become bodybuilders, and remain true to the iron game for life. They know what they want, and pursue it with a passion.

<u>Weak mind = weak body</u>

It goes hand-in-hand. We have either been there ourselves or have been exposed to someone who is. What am I or whom am I referring to? Those that always "talk the talk" but never "walk the walk". It has been my experience on several occasions to meet someone who has a definite desire to get fit and achieve goals. They discuss how and what they will do to get there and, of course, look for your advice as to whether it is a valid approach.

I have personally contributed a great amount of time discussing these or similar things with those that aspire to realize their goals. Following the discussions, you get the feeling that the time was very well spent and that person is going to dedicate time and effort, using some of the knowledge they acquired from you, to realizing their ultimate goal. Not only does it make you feel good inside, you reflect on how you made your own commitment and followed it through to a certain point of satisfaction.

You further realize that the fact that you did follow through enabled you to gain the knowledge that you were able to pass on. Unfortunately and more often than not, you discover that the person who you spent time with did not commit to the plan and made no effort to realize their goal. It becomes apparent when, after several months, the person still looks exactly the same! For whatever reason, they have not made an ounce of progress; this can be and is disappointing to the person who gave help with no expectations for return. The feeling is hard to explain but it is a feeling nonetheless. I often have sat back and recalled in my mind those very experiences and thought, "Maybe it's just not for everyone". You know what I mean. The thought that occurred is probably accurate and true or is it?

I don't and never intend to be condescending towards anyone. However, to me many of those that I have described that fail to follow through when given much of the knowledge and tools needed to make the journey less torturous, possess futile minds resulting in feeble bodies. I say a futile mind because of the fact that time was invested providing that person knowledge as well as know-how with little if any results at all. As a result, they maintain or continue to have the same inadequacies or feeble bodies that they expressed such a distain for when seeking your advice!

Fortunately all is not lost for people who have fallen into this type of situation. It does take "realizing" that the situation exists before it can be confronted. It will probably require that a person of trust make it clear to the person that they are futile and feeble. That is the best thing that can ever happen. Realizing it before it becomes a habit. It many times is habit forming and will impact other areas in your life. It may also be a side effect of a pre-existing futile and feeble condition.

Overcoming this habit will most definitely bring about a life-altering change that cannot be taught or learned but only experienced. Making the decision to avoid futility at all cost and committing to realizing your potential will ultimately "result" in gaining strength and removing weakness. I feel that building a better body teaches this best. To build your body, you must be dedicated and committed to realizing a result.

Whatever that result maybe. Realizing that result is ever-present in your reflection. It will motivate you even more as you progress. The end result will be the absolute removal of feebleness and a strong sense of yourself. You will feel more confident, have a greater self-esteem, and most of all, inspire others around you.

Now, put down that bag of greasy chips and look in the mirror. While looking at yourself, **choose 5 things you "can" change. Be very critical yet honest and reasonable. Make sure to write down what they are.** Once you have the list, read, research, and ask questions in order to determine how and what you can incorporate in your daily routine to realize your desired changes. Remember, patience is a virtue. It won't happen overnight! However, with "the right plan", "the right attitude", "and the right commitment" you will see change. You will gain valuable knowledge from the experience that can be applied to everyday life!

"Whatever you do may seem insignificant but it is most important that you do it." - Mahatma Gandhi

How to think more positively

You've heard it before. "Never say I can't." Think positive. It is almost a cliché, right? But how do the things we say, feel, and believe truly affect our lives? Every day you have internal conversations with yourself, and the way that you conduct those conversations will have a tremendous impact on your success. There is much more to positive thinking than "can instead of can't."

What to do for maintenance

One common question I receive is, "What do you do for maintenance?" It always takes me by surprise because the concept is alien to me. Maintenance? Granted, when I started this lifestyle, I would have loved to have some "vacation" waiting for me at the end, and I was certainly thinking about how I would "relax things" when I achieved my peak physique. Along the journey, however, I learned a true lesson in life: there is never any "maintenance".

Consider this: the average adult loses several pounds of muscle as they age. This has been studied in thousands of individuals over decades and as a person reaches their golden years, they begin to lose muscle mass. So what is maintenance? Is it losing muscle mass? I don't think so. Even gaining enough muscle mass to counter-act the natural loss is "progress" in my book. You must train hard, intensely, and consume the right foods in order to just "maintain" your lean mass. The net result is maintenance of your physique, but the training style is far from "maintenance."

The same thing applies to training in general, even for younger individuals. It is well known that the body is quick to adapt to training. **Because the body is so good at becoming efficient, the longer someone trains, the less gains they are likely to make and the more intense their training must become.**

The converse to this is that because of the high intensity of training, most must rest more to recover as their training advances. Lee Haney once mentioned that he would be happy to put on 5 pounds of muscle in a year. Once again, there is no such thing as maintenance. Even doing the same workout will eventually produce fewer results, and send you backwards instead of keeping you at the same place!

What does this have to do with the "I can, I can't" feeling

The question I always have in return is, "Why do you want maintenance?" Inevitably, people become tired of living a certain lifestyle. Whether it is due to boredom, overtraining, or some other reason, it happens. My own father asked me just recently, "Are you still training? It's okay if you aren't, working out is something you do for a while and then take a break from." The problem is that if you are too focused on a specific goal such as "body fat" or "weight" then it becomes easy to hit that goal and slip into maintenance mode. If your goal, on the other hand, is total health, then it must become a lifestyle change because there is no maintenance. You don't reach good health just to fall back out of it.

The people who yearn for the maintenance mode wake up and tell themselves, "I should go workout." This is an inner dialogue and while it may not seem significant, it is. "I should go workout." This implies a sense of "urgency"; it is not a desire, but a need being fulfilled. There may be a negative consequence if the action is not performed, so it should be done. **Instead of positive reinforcement, this borders on negativity.** After weeks of doing something I "should do," I too, would probably want to hit some magical "maintenance" phase so I wouldn't have to do it anymore.

The alternative to this is to work out because you want to. "I want to go workout." This is a subtle change to the inner dialogue, but it makes a tremendous difference. Now, there is no implied consequence for not doing it. It's not a finger wagging in your face, telling you to do something. **It is an inner desire; the action is tied directly to a reward. If you want to do something, there is typically a reward involved.** Whether it is the satisfaction of accomplishment, the great feeling of good health, or some other positive emotion that springs from the activity.

This reminds me of vegetables. Vegetables? When I started to eat healthy, I knew that I should be eating more vegetables. I did not really like vegetables, and the few that I did eat came packaged with a ton of sodium in a can. I yearned for my "free day" and my "breaks" between programs so that I didn't have to eat vegetables. I still sucked them down because I knew I should eat them, but I did not want to eat them.

Somewhere along the journey, I began to enjoy the journey and realize it was about much more than the destination. It suddenly was not just about losing fat, although that was certainly a bonus. It was about living life. It felt good to be in shape. I made a conscious decision to tie the sensation of good health into the activities that blessed me with it. One such activity was eating vegetables. While I was still eating them because I should, and not because I wanted to, I constantly reminded myself that they were part of what helped me become so healthy.

As time progressed, I began to truly appreciate the benefits of vegetables. I studied their composition and learned about phytochemicals and other components that promote good health. I realized that these were something I'd need to eat for the rest of my life, so I'd better enjoy them. I took some steps towards this. First, I moved towards frozen veggies from canned veggies but added my own seasoning and steamed them until they were mush. Then, I simply steamed them less, to acquire a taste for the crisp, raw flavor, and I seasoned them less. With raw vegetables, I started by dipping them in salad dressing. I reduced the amount that I "dipped" and the amount of times that I dipped and eventually acquired a taste for raw vegetables.

I did not by any means reprogram my entire set of tastes. For some odd reason, I still cannot eat raw tomatoes or mushrooms, and I still want to plug my nose when I eat Brussels sprouts. But, for the most part, I enjoy vegetables. I eat them now because I want to, not because I should. And that means they are not a burden to me or something I need to take a break from. In fact, when I have a "splurge" meal, I often find myself enjoying a nice plate of roasted asparagus because I want to.

Your inner dialogue

The same inner dialogue can take place with your training as well. You don't enjoy cardio? Neither did I. I hated it. I did it because I knew I should, but not because I wanted to. Then, a funny thing happened. I had a fight with a hill in my neighborhood. It was one of those straight "up and down" hills that I couldn't quite make it to the top of. Every time I went out to jog, I set my sights on that hill, and every time, it would defeat me. I had all but given up one day when I realized that I was following the same pattern over and over again. I would start to go up that hill, then I'd feel the nausea kick in, then instead of pushing myself to my limits, I would just talk myself into stopping.

While cardio was still something I did because I should, that hill was something I wanted to conquer. So I detached my mind from that feeling I got and instead decided to see what my body was made out of. I felt disconnected from my legs and arms as they slowly pushed me up that hill, but when I neared the top, I knew I had it in me. I refused to let my mind distract me: "Oh, Jeff, wouldn't it be nicer to just stop and walk right now?" I ignored that inner, negative dialogue and pushed through. I conquered it.

The feeling of ecstasy at having accomplished this little task on my own was incredible. I savored it, and then an interesting thing happened; I began to crave it. So the next time I did cardio, I thought about how I could push myself more than I expected. In the past 18 months, this is how every cardio session has been. I don't feel satisfied unless I know I pushed myself to the limit. If I have anything left at the end then I am disappointed. As I step onto my treadmill, however, I realize that things are different now. I'm not stepping on because I should; I'm stepping on because I want to.

Positive lifting

I think it is safe to say that weight lifters have a certain mind-set when they are training in the gym. For example, ever see that guy who paces back and forth before a set, looking at the ground and muttering obscenities at himself? Or, have you ever heard someone say to his training partner "get your mind right" before a set? That's what I mean by having a certain mind-set.

Every lifter focuses their attention on something while training. Many choose to think about all of the stress in their lives, or someone that they don't like, or that asshole that cut them off on the way to the gym. This type of thinking gets them "fired up" for their next set. However, this type of thinking can also be detrimental to overall performance.

What to do

Think about it for a second. What do you do when you think of things that piss you off? You're heart starts pounding, your face gets hot, your attitude sucks, and you take on "out-of-control" actions such as slamming stuff down, yelling, or pacing furiously. Take that rationale and apply to training. As for myself, I have found that if I am having a bad day, and I take that baggage into the gym with me, I have a horrible workout.

This is because when I think of the things that are really bothering me, I begin to lose my form, and things turn sloppy. If I'm pissed, I can't think straight, so my choice of exercises is poor, I don't rest long enough between sets, so I fatigue a lot faster than usual, and on top of that, I look like a goon because of the way that I am acting. Not only do I get a crappy workout, but also I leave even more pissed than before.

If you do not lift with this kind of mind-set, and cannot relate, then here is another example. Take that guy who I mentioned earlier. You know the one that was pacing and cussing before his set. If you've seen this animal, you've probably noticed that his form is poor. He probably slings the weight around by dropping the weight on a negative, or cheating on every movement.

In addition, he's probably yelling throughout his set and pounds the bar before every set. If you've seen this guy for a long period of time, you'll also notice that he has looked the same since the first day that you saw him.

Say what?

Still don't get it? Well, here's another example. If you play, or have played sports, then this example is for you. Take baseball; you don't get fired up or pissed off before you go up to bat or before you wind-up to pitch. You don't pace back and forth like a madman before shooting a free throw shot, and you don't cuss yourself out before running a kickoff return. Instead, you focus on what you need to do in order to get a base hit, make a lay-up, or pass for a touchdown.

Guys who do the opposite, and fall into the mental mind-trap that I have been describing are usually those who don't reach their athletic potential because of their poor mental game. If you don't believe me, then just take a look at the course of the career of a former Atlanta Braves pitcher with the initials J.R.

Having said that, think about the opposite as being the case. Instead of focusing on rage before a lift, try focusing on something else. Think of something like the lift itself, or something that makes you happy. I have tried this, and it has worked wonders. It sounds a little strange to some people, I know, but stick with me. Many benefits have been associated with positive thinking.

Bruce Lee has spoken of "chi", the life energy that is increased by focusing on the self and thinking positively. Chun Do Sun Bup is a form of "ki" training that aims at re-adjusting the mind to arrange it to a state of order and harmony by seeking out sources of disharmony and releasing that energy. This type of training has had beneficial results on psychological and physical states.

Thinking like Bruce Lee

I am not saying that you must train in the style of Bruce Lee or any other Eastern style. I am simply trying to point out the benefits to thinking positively. Obviously, we all know the immediate benefits of good thoughts. Thoughts that make you feel good give you a sense of being superior, like you can accomplish anything. Doesn't it make sense that this type of thinking would benefit you more in situations where you were trying to accomplish something like a hard workout? **If you can focus your mind on positive thinking, I guarantee a better workout. You will walk into the gym with confidence, and you will not be let down by your performance in the gym.**

Even if you are having a bad day, leave it at the door when you walk into the gym. It makes perfect logical sense; you cannot make positive results from negative actions. Of course, if this idea does not sit well for you, I have another solution. Try focusing on the movement of what you are doing. Personally, I think that this should be automatic.

Mechanics of doing it

Focus on the mechanics of what you are doing and where everything is supposed to be positioned during a movement. Visualize the appropriate muscles being trained, and zero in on how to work that muscle. Even during your set, focus all of your attention on the movement itself and what you are doing to fully train that muscle.

Now I'm not saying that getting "fired up" in the gym is out of the question. It's all in how you do it. Doing this is often a result of a good set or trying to get others around you motivated. However, try not firing yourself up by acting like a primate and cussing at yourself. When you walk into the gym, leave your baggage at the door, and who knows, it might be gone by the time you get done. However, if you take it with you, you can be assured that you will still be carrying that baggage when you leave.

<u>Top 10 reasons to never quit!</u>

Let's face it. Most of us have the best intentions when we start a new workout program. "This time I will actually stick to bodybuilding and not quit!" or "Last time I was forced to quit because I was too busy to lift, but this time I am serious!" Something went wrong and we ended up sitting on our lazy butts for six months straight as our muscles went into hiding and our waists expanded.

Everybody has an excuse about why they haven't yet achieved all their bodybuilding goals. Don't feel too bad though. How many really buff and ripped people do you see on an average day while walking around the city? Maybe one or two if any! At least 95% of people are not too good to look at naked. Sticking to a workout or diet plan is hard! Should that be depressing to you? No! It means that once you succeed you will be one of the very few hard bodies around for everybody to be jealous of.

How do you become one of these motivated and dedicated people? It is 90% psychological. Most of the time when you skip a workout or quit your program it is because you were downright lazy. You need to figure out what works for you when it comes to staying motivated for longer than a month or two. In this section I will teach you what works for me and most of the people I know.

Emotions motivate us to want to do things. We feel the need to do certain things or accomplish certain goals. The following lists of reasons to stay motivated are emotional triggers that can help you remember why you wanted to do this in the first place. Most people forget these things 30 minutes before they are supposed to be at the gym. All they can think about is the fact that they are tired and had a long, stressful day.

Yeah, yeah... I know. Bodybuilding is about the healthy lifestyle. It's great that because of bodybuilding you will live longer, feel healthier, have more energy, prevent diseases, decrease stress, and get sick less often and all that other stuff. Let's be truthful for a second. Did you start bodybuilding so that you could prevent some future disease that you might get someday in the distant future?

I seriously doubt it. Here are the real reasons why we started or are starting bodybuilding. Modify this list so it fits your life and print it out. Put it in your car or in your bathroom so you see it every day and read it before you decide to skip a workout or eat fattening foods.

10. Swimsuit season

Just think of the first time you take your shirt off or put on a bikini this summer. Won't it feel great to know that everybody is looking at you? You will pull your shoulders back and stand tall knowing that you are looking good. Seriously imagine this happening. Don't just read this paragraph and go on. Take a minute to make a detailed mental picture and make it last for a few minutes.

Imagine your friends, family and complete strangers looking at you. Think of your favorite beach or swimming area. Just as motivating can be the thought of not working out and then getting into a swimsuit looking as you do now.

9. Some people expect you to quit

Many of us know those people. You tell them that you are starting a workout program and they just roll their eyes. "Yeah, I'll believe it when I see it!" They expect you to fail and never expect to see any changes. They don't think you can do it. You will prove them wrong and you will love to see the look on their jealous faces when you succeed.

Take a minute and right now and create a list of names of these people. It may be one person or it may be many. Write them down and look at these names before deciding to miss a workout!

8. Friends think they are better than you

Some of us were not born big. Some of us are actually pretty puny naturally. Don't you hate the fact that everybody thinks they can kick your ass? Yes, I know this is immature and doesn't really matter but let's be realistic. If you are a guy, this is one of the worst insults to your manhood.

We all know people who just act like they are better because they are buffer or more ripped. Some of these people simply have good genetics and have no reason to feel all high and mighty. You eat one Snickers bar and gain 10 pounds while this person eats fattening crap all day long and still doesn't gain an ounce of fat.

Ugh! How will they feel when they realize that you are bigger and more defined than they are? Laughing in these people's faces will be a new favorite pastime of yours. Write a list of people like this in your life and keep it close by. Do it now!

7. Being strong

One of the top reasons that people workout is to become strong. Superman is my biggest hero. It just feels great when somebody asks you to open the bottle of ketchup instead of the 10 people sitting next to you.

Won't it be great to have people stare as you load the weight on for a heavy set of bench presses? Being able to do weighted pull-ups or dips gives you a feeling of power over your surroundings.

6. Feeling good about yourself

We all know that you don't look much different after one week of working out. Isn't it weird though that you suddenly find yourself flexing in the mirror a lot more often? You walk around just feeling better looking even if you haven't changed at all yet. This self-confidence can extend itself to other parts of your life and make you an overall more successful person.

5. Feel good when you run into old friends

How many people can you name that gained a lot of fat almost immediately after high school? A lot. How many people can you name who are now in better shape? Not many, if any.

We all love to gossip about how we ran into Chad Erickson and couldn't believe how fat he had become. His face was all pudgy and his body looked bloated. Don't let that be you! Be the one who people can't believe how great you look. Let them wonder how you did it.

Write down a few names of people you haven't seen in a while who you will be happy to impress. A good list would include ex-girlfriends/boyfriends, people who used to look better than you and knew it, people from past sports teams that you were on.

4. Succeed in other areas of life

If you have a job where you see new people often, this could be important. Better looking people have a better chance of getting the best jobs, getting promotions, making the sale and being respected. This may not be morally right but it is true.

We naturally trust good looking people. Many people also assume that fat and out of shape people are lazy, dumb, rude and untrustworthy. This has been proven by many studies. Think of how a good personal appearance can benefit you in your current job. Write these thoughts down now and be specific.

3. Have the dream life you always wanted

Most people's idea of the perfect life would be to be rich, smart, good looking, buff, tan and happy. Obviously, bodybuilding can help you become better looking and muscular. Bodybuilding will help you have more energy and feel better about yourself.

These will naturally help you to be more successful in your career. Many people will assume you are better than others based on your healthy appearance. This can all bring you closer to living the life most people only dream about!

2. Going to the gym is fun

After you belong to a gym for a while, you will get to know the people who work there or work out there. You will make friends with people who have your same interest. The gym becomes like a second home to many bodybuilders.

The feeling of lifting becomes an addiction to many bodybuilders. There is almost nothing better than squeezing out that last rep. The feeling of driving home afterwards knowing that you just ripped your muscles a new one is great. Your daily stress slowly fades away.

1. The opposite sex, what else is there to say?

This is the number one reason most people start working out. They want to attract the best looking girls or guys. The first time a hot woman asks to feel your bulging bicep, you will know that every ounce of sweat and pain was worth it.

Do you have a contradictory mindset?

Bodybuilders are a strange breed. Physically, at least, they are unlike most of the population; bodybuilders seemingly stand apart from their societal peers. However, in many cases, tragically, the visible physical difference is the only thing that separates bodybuilders from other members of the general public.

The human experience is one of emotional variation; of joy and despair, potential and peril. In this all human beings are united and share a common humanity. However, people are also united in another way, and often in a way that they do not consciously realize. If they do realize it, they often become too beleaguered by fear and paralyzed by sheer terror to face it. I am writing about contradictions.

A contradiction does not result from faulty logic, as many would claim. Instead, a contradiction results from a lack of logic, because logic is by its nature unable to be faulty. Logic is the art of non-contradictory identification. In this sense, applying logic is very important for the bodybuilder. Logic is the foundation of science.

Calling the sky, "ground" is one example of a contradiction. Something cannot be both sky and ground at the same time, no more than something can be scientific and mystical at the same time, with respect to the same issue, in the same way.

The foundation of logic is: A is A. Put another way; identity is reality. To call an object by an identifying title means that only that single object may be called by that name. Identity is reality; A is A.

This realization allows man, using his senses, to make concrete, real and objective determinations about reality. It allows him to determine specific things about the metaphysical, and presents him with the ability to formulate plans of action with respect to the man-made. However, sadly, the prevailing attitude of modern society with respect to absolute knowledge is: "Don't be too sure! No one can be certain of anything!"

Statements like these lead to confusion and chaos, and provide each person room to invent their own version of the "truth" on any issue they please. There is only one truth, the metaphysical. Anything man-made is susceptible to error and chaos. The man made is not infallible. Proponents of the "no one can know anything for sure" mentality seek to destroy the method by which man determines reality: his mind. If no one can be sure of anything then absolute knowledge is impossible, and thus chaos and confusion rule.

The idea that no one can be certain of anything is clearly false, and is, in fact, a mentally poisonous idea that leads to confusion, chaos, and feelings of helplessness in times of danger, hopelessness in times of despair, and worthlessness in times where action is needed most. Perhaps the psychological phenomenon of belief perseverance was a compensatory action of the evolutionary process. In light of this line of reasoning it may be credibly argued that this is the case.

It is true that certain people cannot determine anything: the deceased. However, if you are human and are alive, and if you have at least one of your five senses intact, you can make certain determinations about reality. If your sense of touch is not degraded or impaired you can, for example, tell for certain whether or not placing your hand in a flame is helpful or harmful to your physical survival. Other examples exist, but I will not list them here.

Many bodybuilders, in fact, try to find the solution to gaining muscle while denying that a solution is possible. In harboring the philosophies outlined above and in holding these inhibiting contradictory thoughts, many bodybuilders bear guilt. In truly believing that nothing can be known for sure, bodybuilders, and their fellows in society, perpetuate the notion that nothing can be known or accomplished (this includes muscle growth).

"Nonsense" you say "bodybuilders do all that they can to gain muscle" you reason. "Besides, this philosophy is all well and good, but it's the stuff of academics, and has no effect on me." To you I ask: Do bodybuilders really do all that they can to gain muscle? Are you sure that they do? And, most importantly, are you certain that these ideas have no impact on your ability as a bodybuilder?

Whether or it is consciously realized, **most bodybuilders have difficulty gaining mass and improving their health because of two conflicting philosophical systems at work within them. These systems are the systems of mysticism and pseudo-science.**

Logical fundamentals

The process of bodybuilding is a physical and psychological endeavor. Make no mistake: bodybuilding is as much about the body as it is about the mind; at least it is if your goal is to experience a return on your investment of blood, sweat and tears.

Because bodybuilding involves the mind and the body, and thus the physical body and the psyche, it is important to realize that physical and psychological laws apply to bodybuilding, as with every other human daily activity. After all, things function according to their nature; they have no other choice. This takes us back to the fundamental tenet of logic: A is A.

All things must, to function, operate within a defined set of established parameters. When objects operate not as they are intended, they malfunction. The rules of a physical objects functioning is determined by its nature. **This being the case, the physical body functions according to the laws of the physical universe; chemistry, physics, biology, etc. The psyche must also function according to its makeup.**

The body

Bodybuilding, aside from being partially psychological, is also a physical endeavor whose chief purpose is to increase protein synthesis within selected muscles in the body, via endocrine system stimulation. Bodybuilding is a scientific endeavor, and it is only by approaching it in this fashion that any gains may be made on a consistent and continual basis.

The two most important questions that a bodybuilder must answer are:

- **Is putting on muscle possible?**
- **How can I come to know the procedure to do it?**

The obvious way of answering both questions is to simply put on muscle. The process of adding body muscle demonstrates that such a feat is possible and that it is possible to come to have knowledge on the method by which it is may be done.

However, some bodybuilders put on muscle by accident. That is, they do certain exercises, experience muscle growth and then are unable to replicate their results at other times. The chief reason for this is that, although they have put on muscle, thus proving that such a feat is possible, they have not yet discovered the methods and procedures by which they achieved this feat.

The scientific method

Discovering the methods by which one may put on muscle is not difficult. In fact, such a system of detection has been in existence ever since Aristotle shone a light on Mans ignorance of the physical universe. This method of detection is the scientific method.

It was mentioned earlier that that many bodybuilders look for ways to build muscle, yet deny that such a feat is possible. How many times have you heard someone lament about how they are not getting any bigger and that it's "impossible" to grow, yet they continue to look for ways to solve the problem?

The sad reality is that many in this state do not realize that they are looking for something that does not exist. You cannot put on muscle and also not put on muscle at the same time. Either the feat is possible and is so according to a discoverable method, or it is not.

The key to eliminating contradictions and conflicts is to employ the scientific method. This method of discovery, based on empiricism, will dispel and debunk limiting mystical thoughts and will allow you to gather data about your training that is correct. This correct information will allow you to derive constructive calculations, which will, consequently, then allow you to develop a plan of action and procedure that will provide your career with direction, and an opportunity for growth.

Logical fundamentals summary

The key to obtaining maximum muscle growth is to place the maximum level of appropriate stimuli upon the body. In fact, bodybuilding does not require any ineffable, mystical qualities. It does require a myriad of psychological and physical processes, each of which must correspond with reality. Each of which must be true and adhere to physical and psychological laws. It is only by recognizing these laws that a bodybuilder can hope to discover the method of continual muscle gains, and continued successes in their bodybuilding careers.

By continually applying the scientific method to bodybuilding endeavors you will see that making continual gains is possible, and that there is a system by which you can make absolute determinations about reality.

<u>**The balancing act**</u>

We have so much to do with so little time. The days are like a blur and only 24 hours to accomplish 32 hours' worth of details. We all have experienced those days when we wish we had just 2 or even 4 more hours. The only problem is that "Father" or "Mother" (depending on your point of references) just does not want to cooperate. We are fortunate live in a society that allows us to try and do things that we make time to do.

What you decide to do in the 24 hours is based on your individual priority. That priority is defined by your attempt at self-actualization or the need to feel a sense of being. As each day comes and goes, those priorities can and will change.

Why change

Why do they change? Everyone has their own reason. Maybe one realizes that what they want is more time with their kids or spouse. Maybe one realizes that, in order to get that long sought promotion, more time at work is necessary.

Maybe one decides to commit to an exercise regimen after discovering they weight twice as much as they did after graduating from high school. All these reasons and more drive our priorities to be re-defined and change. Unfortunately, too often our health is left behind when priorities are defined.

I believe that, as a society, we need to come to realize the importance of health and fitness as a priority. Ask yourself to list all the reasons why you should make your health a priority. Next, make a list of all the reasons why you haven't made your health a priority.

My reasons that I make my personal health and fitness as priorities are:

1. **Makes me feel better about myself.** I feel that exercise is something that I choose to do and all the benefits realized are for me. No one can take that away not matter how they try. It is mine and I control it. My confidence soars and I know I'm doing something that is good for me.

2. **If I don't do it, who will?** It's easy to just live life without the thought of being healthy. No one will even care or tell you to go to the gym. We sometimes find out the hard way.

3. **The challenge.** I'm in a constant state of learning. I make mistakes along the way and, after a little research, I get smarter and master many of the complexities involved in achieving my goals. It takes tenacity and a commitment to try to be better.

4. **Transfer of knowledge to and from others enables me to improve myself.** The chance to engage in conversations with others having similar goals and experiences is exciting. In health and fitness, knowledge can only have value if one knows how to apply it. That application is specific to each individual. Finding the proper application, is what is makes the experience worth every minute.

Finding balance, the importance of self-improvement

You go to the gym day in and day out with that vision in front of you. That vision of where you want to be, where you want to take your physique and ultimately what you want to accomplish with it in the world of bodybuilding. Time comes to slam down another meal, and you do it with the faith that all of this hard work will pay off. Bodybuilding is not a one-hour training session three days a week. It is much more than that. Bodybuilding is 24 hours a day, 365 days a year. No doubt, it is easy for bodybuilding to take over and consume your everyday life and dictate almost every action and thought you make or have.

Are you one of these people?

All too often you meet the "Hardcore Dudes" who live, work, eat, sleep, drink, and breathe bodybuilding. It is the center of their life and nothing else matters. Shamefully, I used to be one of those people. You may be thinking "well what's wrong with that? Isn't that the only way to achieve real success? Or, there's nothing wrong with it, which is just being consistent and dedicated." First let me ask you what your definition of success is.

If you are the common bodybuilder, you probably have some ideal weight in mind at some percent body fat with certain accomplishments and achievements under your belt. That, to you, would be ultimate success. There are ways to be dedicated and consistent, but you must realize that it does not have to be at the expense of other aspects of your life. **You have to always remember what's REALLY important in life. What will create real meaning, real purpose, real fulfillment, and ultimately real true, complete and utter constant and perpetual happiness?**

"What you achieve through the journey of life is not as important as who you become."

Bodybuilding is all about constant self-improvement. It is a great sport that can produce great things. However, bodybuilding by itself is not enough. What a true bodybuilder will do is take those same principles learned from and through bodybuilding and apply it to virtually every other aspect of his or her life. A good-looking physique is great but it will only bring you temporary and sporadic happiness. A physique sculpted towards perfection is good, but a person sculpted towards perfection is even better.

In fact, it is the best! Move every aspect of your life towards perfection just like you move your body closer and closer to perfection. When we have weak body parts, we prioritize and emphasize them. Just the same, when some other area of your life is weak or not up to par you need to put more emphasis and more effort into improving it! Life does not have to be a one-way path down Bodybuilding Road. But I enjoy nothing more than bodybuilding.

The Doctor Says:
Bodybuilding is a form of self-improvement. If you question this, double check the reasons you are lifting weights in the first place. I am sure they have to do with making your life better and not winning a trophy.

I'm sorry to break it to you but it is not the bodybuilding that you are enjoying, it is the personal growth that is resulting from bodybuilding. Haven't you found this to be true in your life? Think of a challenge that you have overcome in the past. What was it? Maybe getting over an illness, maybe passing an important exam, or maybe something more serious like fighting for your life. What was more rewarding, battling with the challenge, or actually overcoming the challenge and moving on? Although the process can sometimes be enjoyable (what feels better than a muscle engorged with blood after an intense set), it is the end result, the constant self-improvement that we're actually after.

Think of how much more enjoyable and fulfilling life can be if you take those principles of self-improvement and goal setting bodybuilding has taught you and apply it to everything negative in your life. Whether it be swearing, drinking alcohol, smoking, watching too much television, not reading enough, spending too much time at work and not enough time with your family, losing your temper often, depression, unethical practices, or whatever it is. There is GREAT untapped satisfaction and happiness to be gained through the process and end result of the improving of one's self.

Take it one step at a time. Set goals for yourself, just like in bodybuilding. Write down an approach to getting where you want to be, just like in bodybuilding. **Take the actions and steps necessary to turn your goal of self-improvement in some area of your life into a reality, just like bodybuilding.**

Find pleasure in your accomplishments, just like in bodybuilding. Realize how much further you can take yourself, and set new goals, just like in bodybuilding. I personally guarantee you that the rewards are there. If you're looking for continual perpetuating happiness in life, the only way to get it is through personal growth.

Have the power to change

Do you truly believe that you have the power to change? Doubt can do many things. I had doubt. I told myself I wanted to become lean. Here, "want" was not powerful enough. Why? I did not think that I should become lean, I just wanted to. But I was only hoping and grasping, a part of me did not think it was truly possible. This creates a negative feedback loop. When you only want to succeed, then subtle decisions affect the outcome.

For example, if you are underneath several pounds of iron in the gym and getting ready to push out another rep, but your arms ache so bad you can barely grip the weight, what are you going to do? If you only want to succeed, but don't truly believe that you can, you might decide that the pain is not worth it. So instead of pushing that last rep, you decide to terminate the set and rack the weights. It's okay, it was just one rep, and it wouldn't have been worth it anyway, right?

What am I asking for? **I just mentioned moving from "should" to "want" and now I have an issue with "want"!** That's right. For certain decisions in your life, it's not enough to want them. You must make them happen. Yes! It's not a possibility, but a certainty. Instead of wanting to obtain your peak physique, understand that you will. When you have made the decision to stop wanting and start creating, then you will cross yet another barrier. When you are underneath that same set of weights, you'll realize that racking them is not an option. Why? **Because you will earn your peak physique, so you**

must get that last rep in. It is worth it, because by pushing 100% each and every time, you will reach your goal.

How I changed my fate

This is what changed my fate. I hoped to reach it, I wanted it, but it just wasn't there. When I started changing my perspective, when I focused on my inner dialogue and changed it, this is when I experienced success. I didn't train because I was supposed to; I trained because I wanted to. I didn't eat healthy because I should; I ate healthy because I wanted to. And I wasn't hoping to build my peak physique; I was doing it. So when I looked in the mirror, I didn't think about what I could become, I thought about what I was becoming. I'd look at my stomach and see the abs I would create, not the ones that I wished I would have.

Only that thin line between "want and will" made the difference between "maintenance" and success for me. I want you to avoid negatives, like "I can't", because I can. I want you to think positive. But I don't want this to just be a mere cliché. The words hold no meaning when they are not backed by action. **The things you say, feel, and yes, even your own, private thoughts are what sculpt your reality.** Every day you have internal conversations with yourself.

The Doctor Says:
The internal dialogue in your head is very powerful. Words are traveling through your subconscious mind at 1500 words/minute. Use this powerful tool to your advantage with positive thoughts!

Instead of letting the doubt creep in, focus on that dialogue and change it. Simply rephrasing your thoughts as "I want to" or "I will" rather than "I should" or "I hope" can make a tremendous difference. **In fact, just changing the way you think may be the one last step for you to your peak physique.**

How to be a bodybuilder

I would like to give you my personal take on what you need to do in order to be a bodybuilder. We have read all the magazines with all the zillions of workouts and millions of nutrition plans and strategies. We have been bombarded with new gimmick supplements and Zone diets that everyone has tried and failed at. We have all went to the grocery store and bought a hundred dollars' worth of special organic soy based foods because they had a picture of some ripped guy in a magazine eating tofu and drinking soy milk. There are two types of bodybuilders:

1. The ones who try out all the different nutrition, training and supplement plan hoping to gain a pound of beef.

2. The ones who stick with what works and use what has been proven by science to work.

I am a #2. My fridge is stocked with a case of eggs, 8 pounds of chicken, salmon, milk and beef. My cupboards are full of rice, oatmeal, grits and potatoes. My counter tops have 4 canisters of protein and the essential vitamins. My dishwasher is full of mixing glasses and BBQ covered plates. To me, bodybuilding is a journey, a very long journey. There is only one way to get there, lifting the heaviest possible weights and eating so much food you keep the plumber in business.

Now, onto my take on what it means to be a bodybuilder. To me it means that you want to be the biggest thing walking the earth, bigger than an elephant, bigger than a bulldozer and you will not stop pounding iron and eating people until you are that big. You'll die before you quit trying to grow. It means that every morning you get up, pee, and start eating your food, being sure to get your protein, carbs and fats. Then you shower and shave, and then you have a shake. Being a bodybuilder you have to have the mentality that food comes first, before chicks, before playing with your friends, before beer, before watching TV, before sex.

At work, they gave me a fridge to put my food in, and when people see me eating, they know to leave me alone, because I will ignore them until I am done eating anyway. They see the veins in my arms and can see my quads through my blue pants. They know I don't mess around when it comes to eating and growing. And they know this because I have made it very clear to them that bodybuilding comes first, and this job comes second. They know that if they let me eat, then I will go above and beyond my duty at the workplace, and I do. It's a tradeoff you see, they let me do what I need to so that I can do what I have to. That is what it means to be a bodybuilder. When the office is having cake for someone's birthday they don't offer you any because they know you won't have it. When your office all goes out to lunch and you are late because you had to grab your Tupperware.

No excuses, no ifs, ands or buts about it. You eat, you grow and everyone knows it. Being a bodybuilder means that every morning when you leave your house you have your gym bag and your food bag. You have your watch set to let you know when it's time to eat, and when it is time to eat, you eat. You don't wait and say you're still full; you jam the food in your mouth.

Gym time: Bodybuilders go to the gym on schedule with a plan. The plan is to lift as much weight as humanly possible, just shy of crushing yourself. You need to lift so much weight that your eyes turn red, you see stars and almost pass out. If you aren't lifting like that, then don't plan on being as big as you can be. You need to know where the best light in the gym is, where all the good spots to stand and make yourself look good are. You need to know which plates weigh 45 pounds and which are a little off.

Being a bodybuilder is more than knowing all the latest fads and gimmicks. It's being thick, veiny, strong as an ox, hardcore and dedicated. You will know when you see a hardcore bodybuilder. He won't be eating a half bagel with cream cheese and banana slices; he will have his head buried in a plate full of chicken and baked potatoes, drinking warm water and not V8. He won't be wearing a Polo shirt either; he'll have a XXL rag that is pretty tight with his traps starting right below his ears. He won't have fancy pants or fancy cars, because all his money goes to buying chicken, not chicks.

It's time to get serious people! Look around, your friend isn't getting bigger because he takes 2 tabs of Guggulbolic, he bongs shots of N-Large 2 and he sips on Pro Blend 55 all day long. Bodybuilding is no joke, it's not easy and not for everyone. Anyone can go to the gym, anyone can bench 300lbs, and anyone can be average.

<u>Make weightlifting fun</u>

From time to time weight lifting can seem to get boring. Always doing the same thing over and over again. It might even cause some of you to quit lifting all together since you got bored of it. Well, let's make sure that never happens. Here are a few tips that might help you to make your lifting experience more enjoyable.

Workout with friends or family

For me this does the trick. I love working out with a few friends. It also increases the likelihood of you showing up at the gym. Make sure that the person or people that you bring have the same goals and interests. That way you two will most likely be doing the same routine and he/she can spot you or help you out when needed.

Expect plateaus

If you feel you have reached a plateau, do not give up it is a natural part of working out. Make sure you change up your exercises, sets, repetitions and order of your workout. You may even want to try a new workout all together to help you break out of it. You just have to stay in there and try to find ways of making your workout more exciting and fun as you go through this plateau.

Don't get down

Every once in a while you might choose to hang out with friends instead of workout. Do not let this get you down. Or else the thought of you not going to the gym might make it harder to get back into it. Just enjoy the decision that you made and hit the gym harder then you were before on your next workout.

Set goals in all areas of your life

Goal setting can be an ultimate way of keeping weight lifting enjoyable. You just have to think in such a way that every time you do go to the gym, you're getting closer to accomplishing you goals. Whether it be to get bigger, lose weight, get tone and everything in between.

Just do it

Once you start to get great results. Then you will see how the hard work and sometimes boredom was all worth it. Just try to make weightlifting exciting as possible that way every time you enter the gym or weight bench in your garage. It will make you feel like $1,000,000.

Conclusion

High-intensity for bodybuilding involves the application of maximum effort to build maximum muscle in minimum time. High-intensity training bodybuilders don't waste energy trying out the latest super routines in the muscle magazines. They don't train "instinctively." They generally don't squander training times with pumping exercises. They don't adopt the attitude that performing a few extra sets will make up for earlier sets that were poorly executed.

Instead, successful high-intensity training bodybuilders focus mostly on compound exercises such as the dead lift, squat, bent over row, leg press, and other heavy movements. These bodybuilders endeavor to gradually build their poundages by adding a repetition or so each workout and/or increasing the weight by small increments as often as possible, because they know that **getting stronger on the big movements is the best way to stimulate real gains in size.** They know exactly what exercises and weights they are going to use when they arrive at the gym. They strive to get the most out of every repetition and every set.

High-intensity training bodybuilding comprises the soundest application of the principles of exercise physiology. It's a methodical, disciplined, uncomplicated approach to physique development. If you are a drug-free trainee interested in maximizing your natural bodybuilding potential, **high-intensity training is the fastest route to your destination.**

Keep volume low and intensity high

Some claim that you must do a certain number of sets per body part to induce muscular growth. While it's true that the volume of work performed is a consideration, if volume were the primary stimulus for growth then marathon runners would have massively muscle legs. Instead, a casual observation of distance runners almost always reveals thin legs that appear nearly devoid of appreciable muscle.

Intensity that is, the amount of effort applied to each set, supersedes volume when it comes to producing results. Coupled with the gradual progression in poundage, intensity is the key to growth. In fact, one set performed at 100 percent intensity is far more productive than 10 sets performed at 75 percent intensity.

100 percent intensity means performing a set until you are unable, despite your most aggressive effort, to squeeze out one more repetition with good form. This is also known as training to muscle fatigue or failure. It is simple in concept but difficult in execution. Most trainees who think that they are training to fatigue actually terminate their sets well before reaching true fatigue, particularly when it comes to heavy leg exercises. The mind gives out before the body.

High-intensity training bodybuilding is based upon the notion that muscular growth is the result of the body's effort to protect itself from the stress of training heavy. **The more intense the stress, the greater the body's protective response.** This is why the highest possible intensity, taking each work set to the point of muscular fatigue, is required for the fastest progress.

Pushing each set to muscular failure is the most efficient way to train because it ensures the greatest numbers of muscle fibers are stimulated within the shortest amount of time and with the lowest possible volume of work. The all-or-none principle of muscle fiber recruitment states that a muscle uses only the minimum number of fibers necessary to complete a given task and that those fibers contract with maximal force. As you proceed through a set, the muscle fibers that initially lifted the weight become fatigued, forcing fresh fibers to assist in continuing the set. By the time you reach muscular fatigue, most or all of the target muscle fibers have been exhausted. Training to fatigue also ensures that you use the heaviest possible weight for the given number of repetitions. Both of these scenarios set the stage for the fastest possible growth.

This begs the question: if one set to fatigue is good, aren't two sets better and 10 sets better still? No. Performing an excessive number of sets of the given exercise will not increase intensity, it increases volume. It's essential to understand that the body possesses a limited ability to cope with the demands of any stressor, including exercise. **The right amount of high-intensity training leads to results; too much high-intensity training leads to overtraining.** Needless to say, muscular growth will not occur in an overtrained body.

Train briefly and infrequently

Once you understand that training as hard as possible ensures maximum growth stimulation, the next point to grasp is that training as briefly as possible ensures the body has the resources it needs to provide growth. Bear in mind that the body's first priority after a workout is to recover the energy expended during that workout. Only after the body returns to its pre-workout state will it begin the process of supercompensation or growth. It stands to reason that trainees should **perform the minimum amount of work required to stimulate growth to preserve enough energy to foster the growth process.**

There exists no ideal workout length or set. These parameters vary among trainees, depending upon the individual genetic makeup, training history, and lifestyle. But it's safe to say that if you're training in proper high-intensity training style, one or two sets of any exercise is plenty, with six sets being the maximum one should perform for any single body part. Less is probably better for most people.

In general, two workouts per week or a workout every three to four days is sufficient for most to make progress. This applies to advanced trainees as well as beginners. In fact, advanced trainees may need to work out even less often than beginners because their increased strength and ability to generate more effort places their bodies under greater stress. Whatever frequency you initially choose, you should **add more rest days between your workouts if you find that you're still tired and sore by the time of your next workout** or if you fail to increase poundages/repetitions regularly.

Train for strength

Imagine that you currently bench press a maximum of 250 pounds for eight repetitions. You spend the next 12 months performing continuous tension, muscle confusion, and other alleged muscle building techniques. At the end of the twelve-month period, you can still bench press a maximum of 250 pounds for eight repetitions. How much muscle to think you'll have gained? The answer is none. Yes, none, even after years' worth of effort.

That's because a relationship exists between the muscle strength and its size. Sadly, many trainees never comprehend this reality. Instead of making a conscious effort to increase their poundages regularly, they fall into the trap of trying every new technique glorified in the bodybuilding magazines. But because they don't get stronger, they don't get bigger.

Don't be swayed by the throng of so-called bodybuilders who perform set after set of an exercise with the goal of achieving a maximum pump. **A pump has nothing to do with true growth; it is merely a temporary state in which the muscle is engorged with blood.**

If you want to build real, lasting muscle tissue, you must make the muscle stronger. This means training for strength. When you're able to do the target number of repetitions with the given weight, it's time to increase that weight. This increase should be small, about five to ten pounds for leg exercises and 2 1/2 to five pounds on upper body exercises is usually enough.

Most people, when they even bother to increase their weights, make the mistake of increasing them too much. This leads to a rapid deterioration of form. Don't be impatient; overtime, small increases add up to a large increase.

Use an appropriate repetition range

Many authorities believe that hypertrophy can be maximized by repetitions in the range of about 8 to 12. This is a useful principle to follow but, in truth, there can be a significant difference in productive repetition ranges among individuals and among body parts within the same individual.

In general, sets of about five repetitions or less should be avoided by bodybuilders because such low repetitions demonstrate strength rather than build it. In addition, sets of about five repetitions or less at a typical cadence heavily stress the joints and connective tissue without keeping the muscle fibers loaded long enough to provoke growth. Sets of about 15 repetitions or more promote greater metabolic and muscular endurance adaptations rather than strength/growth. **This leaves a usable repetition range for bodybuilding purposes of about 6 to 15.**

A compelling amount of evidence suggests that the lower body responds better than the upper body to higher repetition ranges. As such, it may be best use about 10 to 15 repetitions for lower body work and about 6 to 10 repetitions for upper body work. Experiment with both the upper and lower end of these repetition ranges to discover what works best for you.

Focus on the major muscle groups

If you want to get bigger, you are going to have to pay the price in the form of agonizing effort on exercises that allow you to use relatively heavy weights. The focus should be on compound movements that works several muscle groups at the same time, such as the squat, deadlifts, chin up, bent over row, and bench press. In fact, a very productive routine that stimulates serious growth from head to toe can be built around just these five exercises.

That's not to say that calf raises, arm exercises, and abdominal work should be avoided. They can be part of your program, especially once you're an advanced trainee. Just understand that you'll simulate more biceps growth by doing heavy chin-ups and rows than you will by doing set after set of concentration curls.

The majority of the muscle mass on your body is found in your hips, legs, back, and chest. The only way to gain the pounds of muscular body weight that will accentuate your appearance is by increasing the size of these muscles. **Train the large muscle groups heavy and hard and the smaller groups will gain as well.**

Use proper training style and technique

For best results, it's not enough to lift heavy weights, you must lift them properly. Heaving, thrusting, jerking, and bouncing should be avoided at all costs. As a bodybuilder, your mission in the gym is to exhaust your muscles so that they are forced to rebuild larger and stronger. Weights and machines are the tools you used for that purpose. While you want to lift as much weight as possible for given number of repetitions, you want to do so within the context of proper form.

Jerky and bouncing motions may allow you to lift more weight than you otherwise might be able to handle but such motions minimize the load on the muscles you are trying to work. **Such motions also multiply the stress on your joints and connective tissue, setting you up for injury.**

Some training authorities suggest following a 2 to 4 protocol in which the positive motion takes two seconds in the negative motion takes four seconds. This is fine general advice but what's important to remember is that you want to keep the muscle loaded throughout the entire repetition. Lift the weight with power, precision, and focus; pause for second in the fully contracted position; and lower the weight reasonably slowly while feeling the muscle resist the weight all the way down.

Emphasize recovery more than you think you should

Training provides the stimulus for growth but the growth process does not take place while you train. It takes place later when you rest and especially when you sleep.

Taking an adequate number of days off between workouts is only part of the recovery equation. You must also ensure that your rest days are truly rest days. **If your goal is to add substantial muscle to your frame, minimize your activity level outside the gym.** Playing full-court basketball may be fun but doing so regularly will deplete energy that would otherwise be directed toward recovery and supercompensation. Determine your priorities and act accordingly.

Nor can you afford to frolic until the wee hours of the morning if your dream is to get big. Sleep is critical to the growth process and must not be overlooked. Six hours a night is the bare minimum you should sleep and seven or eight hours is preferable. **Understand that even the most painstakingly devised and religiously followed training program will yield little or no gains if you're sleep deprived.**

Eat well and often

If training serves as the catalyst for growth and sleep provides the opportunity for growth, and food provides the raw materials required for growth.

The ideal eating plan to get big is based around lean protein sources (lean beef, chicken breast, turkey breast, fish, egg whites, and low-fat dairy products), complex carbohydrates (oatmeal, brown rice, yams, and potatoes), fibrous carbohydrates (vegetables and whole fruits), and a small to moderate amount of healthy fats (egg yolks, vegetable oils, nuts, and nut butters). The occasional addition, perhaps a few times weekly, of sweets and fast foods is fine, but keep in mind that a steady intake of sugar and fat laden foods can lead to a rapid accumulation of body fat.

Structure your eating plan to provide five to seven moderate size meals each day. **Smaller, more frequent feedings provide your muscles with a constant supply of the nutrients** they need for growth without promoting excessive fat storage. Such an eating plan will keep your energy level stable and minimize cravings.

Supplements such as protein powers and meal replacements should be viewed as conveniences rather than necessities. Natural food should form the cornerstones of your nutrition program, but when time is short a meal replacement or protein drink is preferable to fast food or no food.

Combine machines and free weights

The arguments in supporting both free weights and machines are loud and long. Free weight supporters claim that the balance required to lift free weights provide a stronger growth stimulus to the muscles and machine lovers point out that machine users can work their muscles harder precisely because they don't have to balance the weight. Free weights are said to be a more natural form of resistance while machines are designed to make up for the inherent shortcomings of barbells and dumbbells.

Each side as valid arguments, so why not get the benefits of both by combining free weights and machines in your program? A very productive routine can be designed around barbells, dumbbells, and whatever machines you have access to.

Keep a daily workout record

Most trainees have no idea where they're going to reach their destination because they don't keep track of where they've been. That is, they don't keep a training diary.

To make the most out of high-intensity bodybuilding, you're going to have to keep records. Don't trust your memory; put your performances on paper. For every work set completed, you should write down the weights used and repetitions obtained. Refer to your training diary during your next training session and try as hard as possible to better your previous performance.

This implies, of course, that the only frequent changes in your routine should be in repetitions and poundages, not exercises. While some variety is reasonable, continually changing exercises doesn't give you the benefit of establishing linear progression from workout to workout, which is the basis for long-term improvement. This does not mean you should use the same exercises for years on end. It only means that you should stick with a given exercise until it ceases to work for you. Leave the so-called instinctive training principle, which states that one should "confuse" the muscles by constantly changing exercises from workout to workout, for those who are more interested in being a Poser than in making progress.

Diet to obtain muscular definition and low body fat

While getting bigger is the primary goal of the typical trainee, most serious bodybuilders eventually develop the urge to improve their muscular definition. After all, the source of the unique appearance of bodybuilders, the thing that distinguishes them from just another big person who pumps iron is crisp, sharply delineated musculature.

In truth, training for definition is a fallacy. **Definition is not a quality that can be trained into a muscle; it is nothing more than the absence of fat over a well-developed muscle.** The peaks, valleys, separations, and veins that characterize a detailed physique exist in anyone who has developed a respectable degree of muscle mass. If these muscular details cannot be seen, it's because they are obscured by body fat.

The best way to train for definition is to adopt a sensible fat loss plan. Put simply, you'll have to eat less. But you want to eat only a little less, starvation diets burn more muscle than fat. A slight reduction, perhaps 300 to 400 calories daily, should be sufficient to set the fat loss machinery in motion. Aim for a loss of just one pound weekly; more rapid weight loss will quickly eat into your hard earned muscle mass.

The best fat loss diets are based around frequent feedings. Eat five to seven small meals a day consisting of lean protein, a moderate amount of carbohydrates, and a small model fat. While mainstream nutritionists typically promote high carbohydrate eating plans, many competitive bodybuilders find that they get their best fat loss results by consuming a moderate amount of carbohydrates, perhaps 40 percent or less of their calories. These bodybuilders also find a better to taper their carbohydrates as the day goes on by eating starchy carbohydrates for breakfast and lunch and fibrous carbohydrates such as broccoli, a staple source of carbohydrates for bodybuilders, during the late afternoon in the evening.

A moderate amount of cardiovascular activity can assist in fat loss. Whether you choose to run or walk at a fast pace outdoors or indoors on a treadmill, or bike indoors or outdoors, or use one of the numerous cardio machines available at commercial gyms. **Start out by performing the activity two or three times weekly for 20 minutes at a moderate intensity.** Gradually increase the duration and number of cardio sessions. Since excessive cardiovascular work can cut into muscle size, perform the minimum amount of cardio activity required to keep fat loss occurring until you reach her goal. Try not to exceed five 45-minute cardio sessions weekly.

While trying to get lean, your approach to weight training should be the same as when you're striving to add mass: train intensely, briefly, and infrequently. At this point, increasing your volume is an even bigger mistake than it was when you training for size, as a decrease in caloric intake and the inclusion of cardio work makes you more susceptible to overtraining.

What about developing an impressive "six-pack" abdominal region? This again is a matter of eliminating excess body fat through diet and cardio. Performing countless crunches, setups, and leg raises in hopes of bringing out the abs is a waste of time and effort. As your percentage of body fat lowers, your abs will become more prominent. **To display a truly impressive rock hard mid-section, you'll need to lower your percentage of body fat too well under 10 percent**, and undertaking that requires discipline and diligence. **Women would need to drop their percentage of body fat to the low teens.**

<u>Questions and answers</u>

I get bombarded with e-mails from all over the world, from Japan to Argentina, and it's interesting to see how small differences there are, really. Everybody wants to know how to get stronger and more buff. Everybody wants to lose body fat. Everybody wants to know if protein drinks really work. The last question is a simple "yes," but the two before that are little bit trickier.

Still, there are some more specific questions that inevitably pop up from time to time. Here are a few of them.

Q: My friend has really peaked biceps while mine are not, while we both curl the same weight. How come? What can I do to increase my peak?

A: Unfortunately, the shape of muscle is largely determined by genetics, so blame mom and dad. However, there are some things you can do. The biceps consists of two separate heads, and by smart training you can develop both to their limit. Don't expect to be able to solely pinpoint one of the two, but you can shift the focus a little. One exercise I have found particularly well for bringing out the peak is bicep curls with a straight barbell, where you hold the bar with a more-than-shoulder-width grip and tuck in your elbows against your sides. Experiment a little to see what works best for you. Start with slightly less weight than usual and do 12-15 reps just to feel where the burn materializes. Then flex your biceps in a classic bicep-pose and use your other hand to squeeze the peak of your biceps. If that's where the lactic acid burn is at, you've found an exercise that will work.

Q: I have a horrible sweet tooth, but I need to get in shape. What can I do to avoid going crazy?

A: Use the window of opportunity immediately after your workouts to have a handful or two of candy. As I've talked about before, that is the one time when you should be eating something sugary to get your body back into an anabolic state again. Make sure to get something sugary though, not fat. Fat has a lot more calories per gram than sugar, and fat will slow down the release of the sugars into your blood stream. Examples of good candy: Jelly beans, sugar babies and reduced fat cookies. Examples of bad candy: Chocolate, candy bars and peanut-butter cups.

Q: You say I should do lat pull-downs to the front rather than behind the neck. Why?

A: To work the lats effectively, you must keep your back slightly arched. By pulling the bar to the front, you're all but guaranteed to keep the arch, while a pull behind the neck lends itself to cheating as you get tired. Thereby you could routinely rob yourself of the benefit from the last few reps of each set without even knowing it. In addition, it's a more natural movement to pull the bar to the front. Your shoulders are at less of a vulnerable angle, and as you get stronger you might avoid cumulative shoulder injuries. This is only true for some people, but the bad news is that you usually don't know if you're one of them until it's too late, so play it safe and assume that you are.

Last but not least, there is an important thing to notice about the lat pulls to the front. You might be tempted to lean back too much when you get tired, thus giving yourself an extra pull. Try to avoid this kind of swaying - sit upright with a lightly arched back, and stay that way throughout the exercise.

Q: What are your thoughts on sports drinks such as Gatorade, Hydra Fuel and such?

A: I don't have any problem with them as long as they're consumed in conjunction with hard and prolonged exercise. Most sports drinks are full of sugar and are formulated to replace lost fluid through sweating, so they're not suitable for drinking with your dinner. In the gym or on a field, they're perfectly fine. Just watch for artificial ingredients. If the drink has a long laundry-list of suspicious-sounding chemicals that you can't even pronounce, pick something else.

Q: My friend is considering buying some steroids, but is concerned about getting ripped off rather than getting the real thing. Is there any web site that can help you identify the legit labels and such?

A: Uh-huh. And I bet your "friend" is about your age and height too, right? Look, here's another reason not to take steroids: It's virtually impossible to know what you're taking. If the crook peddling this dope fills a vial with liquid cleaning agent and slaps a realistic-looking sticker on it, you wouldn't have a clue of what you injected until you woke up in the E.R. If you're lucky, that is. I've seen sites where they promise to show you the telltale signs of counterfeit labels, but guess what? The counterfeiters read the same advice! The bottom line is that all you have to go on is the word of the seller, and, quite frankly, do you think he cares more about your health than his own wallet? Really?

Q: I just can't seem to hit my rear delts properly, and that is getting more and more of a problem as my side and front delts grow. What can I do?

A: Try attaching a handle to the lower pulley on a pulley machine. Then kneel on the floor with your side turned to the pulley. Grab the handle with the hand furthest away from the pulley and lean forward so that you support your upper body with your free hand against the floor. Let the handle pull your other arm so that you feel a good stretch in the rear delt. In other words, if you got your right side facing the pulley, you hold the handle in your left hand while supporting yourself with the right hand on the floor. You should be so far away from the pulley machine that you have resistance even at your most stretched. Then simply pull the handle out to the side as far you can without moving or swaying the rest of your body. The only thing moving should be your shoulder and your arm. This way you can experiment with different angles and slight variations to hit the rear delts 100%.

Q: How important is warm-up, really? I know I'm supposed to do at least 5 minutes on the bike before I hit the weights, but I have very little time...

A: Let me put it this way: If you can "afford" 5 minutes more of watching TV, or 5 minutes of dozing after lunch, or whatever, you'd be better off spending those 5 minutes on a warm-up. Not only do you get your body going so that it utilizes fat for fuel better, it also drastically decreases your risk of injury - especially if you're planning on lifting big.

There's no justification for skipping something that can do so much for your health and safety, unless you're a top-level executive who sleeps 3 hours per night and makes 15-minute appointments to play with your kids on the weekends. If you're a mere mortal like the rest of us, who spends a few hours in front of the tube now and then, you're making an active choice to watch TV instead of looking out for yourself. And by the way, don't you think a single torn muscle, with all the handicaps and rehab it involves, makes up for the time you'd save by skipping the warm-up during your entire life? Play it safe - always warm up.

Q: How come the people in before and after-pictures in the ads always look so much better than I do, no matter how hard I work out, diet, and take the supplements they push?

A: And drinking certain brands of soda doesn't make you an extreme-sporting mega hunk either, even if their ad implies so. Read the fine print. There's always a puny little disclaimer saying something to the effect of: "Mr. Ripped on the picture experienced exceptional results. The typical user may not expect similar results." In plain English, that means they all but admit that while the dude on a picture is a nice fairy tale, the Muscle Fairy will most likely visit not you. The sad truth is that there are no shortcuts. When an ad claims that their product is 3,463% better than the competition, it does not mean you'll gain muscle 3,463% faster. In fact, most scientific claims I've seen are taken out of context. Sure, a certain ingredient in product X may do a lot of good for an 80-year old female diabetic, or help an obese lab rat, but to expect even remotely the same results in a 230 lb, 25-year old male bodybuilder is ridiculous. Yet, they can quote the scientific study and advertise it to create the illusion that the 80-year old woman figures somehow applies to you. It's dirty, but it works. Otherwise they wouldn't keep doing it. Of course, there are honest facts in ads, and there are reputable companies who don't try to scam you with inflated claims, but it's generally easy to spot the difference. Remember: If something sounds too good to be true, it usually is.

Q: I have kind of an embarrassing problem... I don't use steroids, and still I've noticed my pecs are kind of "drooping" when relaxed, making them look like the beginning stages of breasts. I train religiously, I have very little body fat, and still I think it keeps getting worse! What's up with this??

A: Don't panic. What you're seeing is probably the effect of too much decline bench pressing. Lately, I've seen a surge the number of people using decline presses, the kind where you lock your legs between two rolls and lay with your head down on a declining bench. This often allows you to use slightly more weight in the bench press, which as we all know is the Holy Grail for 99% of the male gym rats ages 15 to 30. The bad news is; the pectoralis major has a fan-shape, allowing you to train different areas to different degrees. If you do a lot of incline presses, you're weaker compared to the flat press, but you train the upper part of your chest. This gives you a well-balanced, rock-solid look. However, if you train the lower part of your pecs too much, especially if neglecting the upper part, you grow the muscles into looking like a flat-chested dude with beginning bitch tits. Make sense? The muscles will grow according to how you train them, so my advice to you is to stop doing decline presses immediately, and focus on flat and incline presses for a couple of months. When you've balanced out and start feeling comfortable again, you can go back to a normal training routine again - splitting the focus equally between the upper and lower part of the chest.

Q: Why is breakfast so important?

A: When you've been asleep for 8 or so hours, you haven't eaten for at least 8 hours, possibly more like 10 or 11 hours. This means your body is really low on amino acids and carbs, both something you want to have floating around in your body to stay anabolic. The best way to break the starvation of your muscles is to have a hearty breakfast as soon as possible as you wake up. Also, if you work out early in the day, it's extra important to get a lot of carbs with your breakfast, as you'll need it to fuel your workout.

Q: What is the best repetition range for building muscle?

A: At an average repetition cadence (speed), generally 8 -12 reps per set will elicit the greatest gains in lean mass. Sets consisting of less than 6 or 8 reps generally focus on muscle strength, whereas a high number of reps each set targets muscle endurance.

Detailed Answer:

The conventional view that fewer reps in each set equates to more muscle gain is a bit too simplistic. In reality, when one performs sets with very high weight and low reps, the main physiological change is a strengthening of neuromuscular pathways. In other words, high weight/low reps strengthen the brain's ability to activate muscle. However, if we bump up the reps slightly while decreasing the weight as necessary, the muscle tissue will perform more total work, and thus more muscle growth will occur. However, if the reps are increased too high, the main effect will be an increase in muscle endurance.

Through research, it has been determined that the best range for hypertrophy (muscle gain) is roughly between 8-12 reps. As the reps are decreased from this range, the program will elicit greater strength gains will less size. In contrast, more than 12 reps mainly allows for increases in muscular endurance.

Q: Does weight training cause high blood pressure?

A: Natural bodybuilders are among the most fit individuals in athletics. While weight training itself has little effect on cardiovascular health, it does not increase blood pressure in the long term. Although blood pressure does rise during any type of exercise, which is not dangerous for healthy individuals. However, most bodybuilders also engage in cardiovascular exercise, which is well established for decreasing blood pressure.

Also, natural bodybuilders tend to be very lean; not only on the "outside," but also on the "inside," as they tend to have less fatty plaque lining artery walls, and are therefore at a reduced risk for atherosclerosis. Further, the "large heart syndrome" that many purport as a result of weight training has not been proven in research.

Q: Is it possible to gain muscle strength or muscle endurance without gaining muscle size?

A: It is possible to gain strength without increasing muscle size (hypertrophy). Similarly, it is possible to enhance muscle endurance without hypertrophy. However, it may be difficult to train for both goals at the same time.

- Training for muscle endurance is generally achieved through high repetitions and lighter weights.

- To train for strength while minimizing gains in muscle mass, it is advisable to perform low repetitions per set, using explosive movements (short concentric contractions) while lowering the weights under control. Be sure to be adequately warmed up before starting into the working sets.

Detailed Answer:

Training for strength over size is largely attained through manipulating the neuromuscular system (brain-muscle connection); that is, strengthening the nervous system as a muscle "activator". As a protective mechanism for the body, the central nervous system has safeguards in place that shut down muscle activity when the muscle attempts to work at too high an intensity.

Specifically, one of these systems works through an organelle found in tendons of muscle, which shuts down muscle activity when it senses that there is too much strain on a muscle. Also, for the untrained individual (or somebody who rarely lifts very heavy weights), the connection between muscle and brain may be relatively weak. To train the neuromuscular connection, it is advisable to perform low repetitions per set, using explosive movements (short concentric contractions) while lowering the weights under control.

Be sure to be adequately warmed up before starting into the working sets. Although muscle fiber density may increase from this type of training, hypertrophy is minimized since high resistance/low rep training does not elicit changes in extra-fibril structures (blood vessels, organelles like mitochondria). At the same time, strength gains will be evident through neuromuscular manipulation.

Training for muscle endurance is generally achieved through high repetitions and lighter weights. With this type of training, the major change to the muscle is the ability to manage metabolic waste, and fuel utilization. For example, the muscle is better able to utilize lactate as a fuel rather than allow it to minimize muscle performance.

Also, more efficient fuel sources such as fats make up a larger portion of the muscle's fuel. Rather than carbohydrates which tend to promote metabolic waste accumulation. Note, however, that some of these changes include increased capillary (and blood vessel) density and mitochondria, changes that reduce muscle density. Nevertheless, these changes will not cause a significant increase in muscle size.

Since these two goals require quite different methods of training, a good approach may be to periodize your training. That is, train for muscle endurance for 3-4 weeks, and then switch to a training program geared towards building muscle strength.

Q: What is meant by the term Basal Metabolic Rate?

A: Basal Metabolic Rate (BMR) or basal metabolism represents the minimal energy expended to keep a resting, awake body alive. This requires about 60-70% of the total energy use by the body. The processes involved include maintaining a heartbeat, respiration, temperature and other functions. It does not include energy used for physical activity or digesting foods. Basal metabolism accounts for roughly 1 kcalorie/kilogram (2.2 lbs.)/hour. I use the term 'roughly," due to the fact that the amount of energy used for basal metabolism depends primarily upon lean body mass.

Q: What causes delayed onset muscle soreness?

A: The cause for delayed onset muscle soreness (DOMS) has been debated at length by exercise physiologists, and is still not fully understood. Mechanisms for theories proposed in the past have included lactic acid buildup, torn tissue, muscle spasm, and connective tissue damage. Of these, the lactic acid buildup theory, and spasm theory have largely been discounted by exercise physiologists. Currently, the most accepted theory for DOMS seems to be muscle/connective tissue damage due to mechanical forces on the muscle and connective tissue.

Q: I heard that exercising on an empty stomach leads to losses in lean body mass. Should I really be exercising on an empty stomach?

A: There are benefits to working out on an empty stomach, and different benefits when one works out after eating. Ultimately, one should choose the method based on their fitness goals. As a rule of thumb, it may be best to perform workouts on an empty stomach if one's main goal is body fat loss. However, if one is only concerned with gaining lean mass, eating 30-60 minutes before a workout may be a good idea.

For people looking to lose body fat while increasing muscle mass at the same time, it may be best to take advantage of the key benefits of each method. For example, one could try working out on an empty stomach some days, and eat 30-60 minutes before working out on other days (i.e. eat before resistance exercise sessions; do not eat before cardio). Following is a detailed breakdown of the benefits and drawbacks to each method:

Eating 30-60 minutes before a Workout

Benefits:

- Maximizes liver and muscle glycogen, a fuel stored in muscle that is necessary for intense exercise (assuming that the meal is balanced).

- Prevents the breakdown of muscle tissue (by preventing the secretion of the hormone cortisol).

- Allows for longer duration workouts.

- May increase secretion of growth hormone (particularly with exercise that elicits high lactate production, like intense cardio) therefore greater utilization of fat as fuel, free fatty acid (FFA) release, and protein synthesis.

Drawbacks:

- Suppresses FFA release from fat stores (due to the presence of insulin).

• Excess insulin (which easily occurs through eating too many calories or high glycemic foods) may cause hypoglycemia, leading to depleted muscle glycogen stores therefore exerciser "crashes".

Exercise on Empty Stomach

Benefits:

• Increases FFA availability in blood therefore increases the amount fats burned as energy.

• May increase secretion of growth hormone (particularly with exercise that elicits high lactate production, like intense cardio) therefore greater utilization of fat as fuel, FFA release, and protein synthesis (note that this is an unresolved issue, as it contradicts the bullet above).

Drawbacks:

• Increased production of cortisol therefore leads to the breakdown of muscle tissue.

Q: On certain training days such as when I do back and biceps together, sometimes it is difficult to hold onto the bar because of forearm fatigue. Is there anything I can do to correct this?

A: Forearm strength is often a limiting factor, especially when handling heavy weights vertically such as pull-ups or deadlift. Chalk, sticky pads, or weightlifting straps can help with handling the load when necessary, however, as a rule of thumb, it is best to work through this discomfort since these very activities are some of the best exercises for developing the forearms and building grip strength. On the contrary, straps and chalk should always be used.

When to use straps and chalk:

1. Your ability to hold the weight compromises the safety of the movement, or

2. Lack of grip strength limits your ability to strengthen/develop the target muscle effectively.

Q: I have had a cold the past couple of days and was wondering if it is a good idea to still exercise?

A: You may think it is a good idea not to engage in vigorous exercise when you have the sniffles. However, a new study suggests that if you are well enough to get out of bed, you are probably well enough to get a workout. Researchers at Ball State University in Indiana found that exercising does not delay recovery or worsen symptoms of the common cold.

In the study, 34 moderately fit folks, ages 18-29, were assigned to an exercising group, while 16 additional people of similar age and fitness level were assigned to a non-exercising group. Then both groups were inoculated with a virus to produce upper respiratory illness. The exercising group worked out at 70% of maximum heart rate for 40 minutes per day, every other day.

Researchers collected used facial tissues and administered symptom questionnaires every 12 hours to gauge the progress of the illness and its symptoms. After ten days, analyses of symptoms were similar between the exercising and non-exercising groups. So while you may feel like scaling down your routine if you are feeling under the weather, there seems to be no reason to skip it altogether.

Q: I've heard the terms "concentric and eccentric contractions." What do these mean?

A: A concentric contraction occurs during the lifting phase of an exercise, when the muscle shortens or contracts. For example, when you lift the weight in a bench press, pressing it from your chest to the lock-out position, that is the concentric, or "positive," phase of the exercise. An eccentric contraction occurs during the lowering phase of an exercise, when the muscle lengthens. For example, lowering the weight to your chest during the bench press is the eccentric or "negative," portion of the exercise.

Q: What can I do about 'stretch marks' that appear after I've been weight lifting and gaining size and strength?

A: If you are weight training and gaining some size and muscularity, chances are you will begin to develop stretch marks. This is, to a certain extent, unavoidable. You may minimize their development, however, through the application of a topical antioxidant cream that contains collagen. Regular application of this type of lotion/cream will increase skin elasticity, and thus diminish the formation of stretch marks, but it may not fully prevent their development.

Q: What can I do to prevent muscle cramping?

A: Muscle cramping occurs when a muscle continues to contract, and cannot seem to "let go". The painful sensation one feels is caused by muscle fatigue, and waste products like lactic acid that build up in the muscle. Although the cause of muscle cramps is not entirely understood, a number of factors seem to be involved, including hydration level, electrolyte balance, training history, and chronically tight muscles.

Some factors that may increase muscle cramps:

1. Training history seems to be the most important factor. Exercise beyond an accustomed limit (longer duration, or intensity) will often bring on muscle cramps. However, through regular training, one tends to experience muscle cramps less frequently.

2. Make sure that you are drinking enough water - 10 glasses of water daily (at least 10 oz. each), or if you care to be more precise, 0.6oz/water/lb. of bodyweight. Increase this amount if you consume caffeine. For each cup of coffee, tea, or soda you take in, please be sure to add an additional 10 oz. glass of water for each.

3. Through sweating (especially in a hot environment), one tends to lose electrolytes like sodium, potassium, and magnesium. Normally these are replaced in the diet. However, prolonged exercise (longer than 1 hour) in hot environments may create a need for mineral replenishment. Try adding a bit of salt to your foods, and take a multivitamin/mineral supplement and see if this makes a difference.

4. Lastly, tight muscles are best addressed by stretching before and after every workout. Stretching allows more nutrients, blood, etc. into the muscle, and allows you to dispose of waste materials more easily due to increased blood flow.

Q: What is the current theory on using a weight belt? Should I or shouldn't I use one?

A: Weight belts are a handy tool for helping to protect your back on those lifts that may stress it, but that does not mean you should use them on every lift for every rep. When you do an intense exercise that involves the back, such as squats, it would seem logical that you would want that safety precaution in place at all times.

In doing so, however, you may predispose yourself to an injury by taking the muscles that would ordinarily act as natural back supports out of the equation. Essentially, when you are doing a squat, your primary focus in terms of strength is your leg muscles. What most people don't realize is that you are also simultaneously strengthening your back support muscles; abdominals, lower back, obliques, etc.

When you wear a belt, you take those muscles (to a lesser or greater extent depending upon form) out of the chain, and as such they do not get strengthened to the same degree as do your leg muscles. What this may do in the long run is create an imbalance in the body in terms of overall support and equilibrium, which as you continue to grow stronger and use more weight, may increase the risk of injuring yourself in one way or another.

Perhaps the best way of looking at these muscles is to consider them a chain, and as you know, a chain is only as strong as its weakest link. As such, if you're going to strengthen any part of the chain, you better strengthen the whole chain to keep yourself safe and prevent injuries. When would you want to use a belt? Usually, the only time to use a belt is when you are attempting a maximal lift; anywhere from 4 - 6 reps of a challenging weight that involves back support and all-out effort. At all other times, it's a good idea to simply use good form and have a competent spotter on these exercises.

Q: I have been told all of my life that you have to work out at least 30 to 35 minutes in order to begin burning fat. Is there any scientific data you can provide to prove that the 20-minute aerobic solution does in fact burn fat?

A: When trying to lose body fat, the duration of the workout is less important than total calorie balance (total calories burned). To lose fat, it is necessary to achieve a calorie deficit. That is, the number of calories you burn must be greater than the number of calories you ingest. Cardiovascular exercise helps you to create this calorie deficit by burning excess calories. Although you can burn calories at any workout intensity, it is most efficient to work at a high-intensity for shorter periods of time compared to long-duration workouts.

For example, working at a high-intensity, one can burn up to 50% more calories in a shorter period of time. More importantly, post workout, you continue to burn calories at an elevated rate up to 142% more than low-intensity aerobics within the first hour following the cardio session. What's more, this elevation in metabolism lasts up to 48 hours post workout, an effect not achieved with low-intensity exercise. The bottom line is that while low-intensity, long-duration exercise is effective for fat loss; typically one sees better results using a high-intensity protocol. Plus, this type of training is more efficient since once spends less time in the gym, but typically experiences better results.

Q: I typically run outdoors, but when it's hot and humid, I head to the treadmill. Does running on the treadmill burn fewer calories?

A: If you're running at speeds under 9 miles an hour (a very fast 6:40-minute-mile pace), treadmill running burns about the same number of calories as running outdoors. But if you run faster than 9 mph, you'll burn fewer calories on the treadmill. The difference can be up to 8 percent because you don't have to overcome wind resistance and because the treadmill belt does propel you along a bit.

Q: A year and a half ago, I started running 5 miles on a treadmill six days a week and lifting weights three times a week. The results have been fabulous; a 74-pound weight loss, a huge drop in blood pressure and an enormous surge in self-esteem. But now my knees ache, especially when I walk downhill. Is this a result of running? What can I do about the pain?

A: Six days a week of high-impact training such as running is very hard on the body, especially the knees. Substituting a low-impact activity such as biking, swimming or the elliptical trainer once or twice a week is much healthier.

Most likely you're experiencing patella-femoral syndrome, also known as pain behind the kneecap. Running, especially on hard surfaces, increases the pressure of the patella (kneecap) on the femur (thighbone) when you bend and straighten your knee.

Q: Is it easier for a man to get six-pack abs than for a woman to?

A: Yes. The appearance of defined, rock-hard ab muscles is possible only if the abs are highly trained and there is very little fat on top of them. On average, women have more total body fat than men, and proportionally they nave more subcutaneous fat. What's more, it's easier for men to lose body fat than it is for women, partly due to hormonal differences. If you put men and women on the same exercise and diet program, men will lose more weight on average. Of course, not every man will lose more fat than every woman will. There are exceptions; some women can achieve a six-pack without tremendous work, and some men have no chance of ever having sleek abs.

The bottom line, don't get frustrated if you can't achieve that six-pack. It may not be a matter of lacking willpower. It could be just a matter of genetic and gender destiny.

Q: I have a friend who does a 5- to 10-minute warm-up on a treadmill, then lifts weights, then does 20 more minutes of cardio. Does her warm-up really count as cardlo? I've heard you need to do 15 consecutive minutes to get benefits.

A: A 5- to 10-minute warm-up certainly would count. Since a warm-up is performed at a low intensity, you won't burn as many calories those first few minutes. But that doesn't mean you're not benefiting. Most people don't need more than two or three minutes to get their heart rate up to the lower end of their target zone. At the lower end of the zone — about 60 percent of your maximum heart rate — your body is working hard enough to achieve health and fitness benefits.

There is no research establishing the minimum number of consecutive minutes necessary to "count," but plenty of research has established the benefits of short cardio bouts.

Of course, if you are training for an endurance event such as a 10k or marathon, 10 minute workouts aren't going to cut it. But for general health and fitness you can break it down, research shows tremendous benefits from performing 15 10-minute exercise bouts per week, including cardio exercise, strength training and stretching.

Q: What happens if I go over my target zone for fat burning?

A: You will burn glycogen (blood glucose), which is fine. The problem, however, is that unless you are a highly trained athlete, you don't have high amounts of glycogen stored in your muscles cells and other storage areas. In this case, cortisol, one of the hormones secreted with exercise begins to break down muscle tissue to transform it into glucose so you can continue to exercise/survive. This process is commonly known as "gluconeogenisis," or the new formation of glucose by breaking down muscle.

Q: Why are strong abdominal muscles so important?

A: A strong mid-section will help support the lower back (lumbar spine). It also helps transfer strength and power from the upper body to the lower. In general, the abdominal muscles, lower back, and pelvic region is called the "core." What you need to strive for is "core stability." When the hip flexor muscles are too tight, it causes inflexibility and forward pelvic tilt. Weak abdominals and a tight lower back will create an excessive arch in the lower back known as "sway back." When an imbalance is present in this area, the result can be pain, poor energy transfer in sports, and general body discomfort. Over time, the result can be spinal segments that lip, spur, and even fuse.

Q: How important is massage therapy to an athlete?

A: In one word "VITAL". Massage does the following: reduces stress, decreases recovery time, promotes healing, increases performance, increases speed, releases toxins and it feels oh, so good! Make sure your massage therapist known your tolerance for pain, what type of massage you've experienced, and your intended benefit from the massage.

Q: Should I stretch before or after I work out with weights?

A: Both. Prior to any stretching, a general warm-up should take place. A bike, rower, treadmill or stepper is fine. This is to heat the body's core temperature. Once the core is warm, perform some moderate intensity stretches. Make certain the entire body is stretched, however spend a little extra time on the specific area you intend on training first. After you finish your lifting routine, your body will be very warm and better able to stretch more deeply. This is the time to gently increase the intensity of your stretching.

Q: If I'm very over weight, should I still lift weights? I don't want to bulk up any more.

A: You absolutely should lift weights. It doesn't need to be your focus, but it needs to be included in your complete program. In most cases, weight training is not cardiovascular in nature. This means your body will not use fat as a primary source of energy while lifting weights. However, weight training does make your body better at consuming calories throughout the day. Because a muscle requires more energy to maintain its structure as compared to fat, your body must use (burn) more calories to maintain that muscles integrity. Aside from all this, if you don't maintain or build muscle as you lose weight, you will become what is known as a "thin, fat person." This is a slightly built person who has no muscle mass.

Q: Is there a difference between types of creatines that are currently available?

A: As some people are aware, you can now find creatine on the market in three forms: phosphate, citrate, and monohydrate. My feeling is that the phosphate variety is not easily absorbed by the body and for this reason will not yield effective and substantial results. The citrate variety seemed to be catching on for a time, but again the research is sketchy here. In fact, nearly all the positive clinical studies that have been done on creatine have utilized the monohydrate form, and this is the only form that I currently recommend.

Q: My doctor told me I am allergic to wheat and dairy products. How could this be? Is there a test or a way to really find out if I am allergic?

A: I think the only way you can find this out is by omitting all forms of those foods from your diet for at least a week, then adding the food back and seeing if your symptoms return. Also, since both wheat and dairy products are found in so many foods, you'll have to read the labels of processed foods especially carefully.

Q: I love chocolate. Is it really bad for you? How much can I eat without sabotaging my healthy eating plan?

A: Chocolate isn't all bad. In fact, chocolate is rich in antioxidants called phenolics, the same compounds in red wine that seem to offer protection against heart disease. And cocoa butter, the fat in chocolate, does not appear to be so bad for your heart and arteries. Its principal saturated fat, stearic acid is converted by the body into oleic acid, a heart-healthy monounsaturated fat also found in olive oil. Pick chocolate made with cocoa butter rather than unhealthy fats such as palm and coconut oils. This means look for cocoa to appear in the ingredients before sugar.

Q: I seem to be addicted to sweets. How do you suggest I stop eating foods high in sugar?

A: Taming your sugar cravings could be a matter of slowly reeducating your taste buds or learning to feel satisfied with less. If you slowly cut back on sweets, you will find that healthy sweet foods taste exceptionally sweet - fresh strawberries, frozen grapes, mangoes, dried unsweetened cherries. Treats like these will satisfy your sweet tooth if you take the time to eat them with full attention to taste, aroma, and presentation.

Q: What are the pros and cons of eating farm-raised salmon instead of salmon from the wild? I've heard farmed salmon is not a good source of omega-3 fatty acids because of what the fish are fed.

A: I always choose wild salmon over farmed salmon. Flesh from most pen-raised salmon may be lower in beneficial omega-3 fatty acids and higher in harmful saturated fats than that from their wild cousins - a consequence of what they are fed. And worst of all, is that the under exercised muscles of salmon reared in cages produce a soft, bland-tasting fish that just doesn't stand up to the wild version. The product label will tell you whether or not the fish was farmed.

Q: What is your take on alpha-lipoic acid?

A: Alpha-lipoic acid (ALA) has a number of admirable qualities including the unique ability to work nearly anywhere in the body. It also appears to be safe, readily converts into a useable form, and neutralizes many different kinds of free radicals. This tiny molecule recycles antioxidants such as vitamin C and E, prolonging their effectiveness.

<h1 style="text-align:center"><u>Terms and definitions</u></h1>

AEROBIC EXERCISE

Prolonged, moderate-intensity work that uses up oxygen at or below the level at which your cardiorespiratory (heart-lung) system can replenish oxygen in the working muscles. Aerobic literally means with oxygen, and it is the only type of exercise, which burns body fat to meet its energy needs. Bodybuilders engage in aerobic workouts to develop additional cardiorespiratory fitness, as well as to burn off excess body fat to achieve peak contest muscularity. Common aerobic activities include running, cycling, swimming, dancing, and walking. Depending on how vigorously you play them, most racquet sports can also be aerobic exercise.

ANABOLIC DRUGS

Also called anabolic steroids, these are artificial male hormones that aid in nitrogen retention and thereby add to a male bodybuilder's muscle mass and strength. These drugs are not without hazardous side effects, however, and they are legally available only through a physician's prescription. Steroids are available in most gyms via the black market, but it is very dangerous to use such unknown substances to increase muscle mass.

ANAEROBIC EXERCISE

Exercise of much higher intensity than aerobic work, which uses up oxygen more quickly than the body, can replenish it in the working muscles. Anaerobic exercise eventually builds up a significant oxygen debt that forces an athlete to terminate the exercise session rather quickly. Anaerobic exercise, the kind of exercise to which bodybuilding training belongs, burns up glycogen (muscle sugar) to supply its energy needs. Fast sprinting is a typical anaerobic form of exercise.

ANDROGENIC DRUGS

Androgenics are drugs that simulate the effects of the male hormone testosterone in the human body. Androgens do build a degree of strength and muscle mass, but they also stimulate secondary sex characters such as increased body hair, a deepened voice, and high levels of aggression. Indeed, many bodybuilders and power lifters take androgen to stimulate aggressiveness in the by resulting in more productive workouts.

BALANCE

A term referring to an even relationship of body proportions in a man's physique. Perfectly balanced physical proportions are in a much-sought-after trait among competitive bodybuilders.

BAR

This is the steel shaft that forms the basic part of barbell or dumbbell. These bars are normally about one inch thick, and they are often encased in a revolving metal sleeve.

BARBELL

Normally measuring between four and seven feet in length, a barbell is the most basic piece of weight-training and bodybuilding equipment. Indeed, you can train every major skeletal muscle group in your body using on a barbell. There are two major and types of barbells used for exercise in common use, adjustable sets; in which you can easily add or subtract plates by removing a detachable outside collar held in place on each side by a set screw. And fixed barbells; in which the plates are either welded or bolted permanently in place. Fixed weights are arranged in variety poundages on long racks in commercial bodybuilding gyms, the approximate poundage for each one painted or etched on the bar. Fixed weights relieve you of the problem of changing plates on your barbell for each new exercise. While fixed barbells and dumbbells are normally found in large commercial gyms, adjustable barbell and dumbbell sets are more frequently used at home.

BASIC EXERCISE

This is a bodybuilding exercise, which stresses the largest muscle groups of your body (e.g., the thighs, back, and/or chest), often in combination with smaller muscles. You will be able to use very heavy weights in basic exercises in order to build great muscle mass and physical power. Typical basic movements include squats, bench presses, and deadlifts.

BENCHES

A wide variety of exercise benches is available for use in doing barbell and dumbbell exercises either lying or seated on a bench. The most common type of bench, a flat exercise bench, can be used for chest, shoulder, and arm movements. Incline and decline benches (which are angled at about 30-45 degrees) allow movements for the chest, shoulder, and arms.

BIOMECHANICS

The scientific study of body positions, or form, in sport. In bodybuilding, biomechanics studies body form when exercising with weights. When you have good biomechanics in a bodybuilding exercise, you will be safely placing maximum beneficial stress on your working muscles.

BMR

The basal metabolic rate is the speed at which your resting body burns calories to provide for its basic survival needs. You can elevate your BMR and more easily achieve lean body mass through consistent exercise, and particularly through aerobic workouts.

BODYBUILDING

A type of weight training applied in conjunction with sound nutritional practices to alter the shape of one's body. In the context of this book, bodybuilding is a competitive sport nationally and internationally in both amateur and professional categories for men, women, and mixed pairs. However, a majority of individuals uses bodybuilding methods merely to lose excess body fat or build up a too thin part of the body.

BURN

This is a burning sensation that you feel in the muscle that you are training. This burn is caused by a rapid buildup of fatigue toxins in the muscle and is a good indication that you are optimally working a muscle group. The best bodybuilders consistently forge past the pain barrier erected by muscle burn and consequently build very massive, highly defined muscle.

BURNS

A training technique used to push a set past the normal failure point, and thereby to stimulate it to greater hypertrophy. Burns consist of short, quick, bouncy reps 2-4 inches in range of motion. Most bodybuilders do 8-12 burns at the end of a set that has already been taken to failure. They generate terrific burn in the muscles, hence the name of this technique.

CARDIORESPIRATORY FITNESS

This is the physical fitness condition of the heart, circulatory system and lungs that is indicative of good aerobic fitness.

CHEATING

A method of pushing a muscle to keep working far past the point at which it would normally fail to continue contracting due to excessive fatigue buildup. In cheating you will use a self-administered body swing, jerk, or otherwise poor exercise form once you have reached the failure point to take some of the pressure off the muscles and allow them to continue a set for two or three repetitions past failure.

CHINNING BAR

A bar attached high on the wall or gym ceiling, on which you can do chins, hanging leg raises, and other movements for your upper body. A chinning bar is analogous to the high bar male gymnasts use in national and international competitions.

CIRCUIT TRAINING

A special form of bodybuilding through which you can simultaneously increase aerobic conditioning, muscle mass, and strength. In circuit training, you will plan a series of 10-20 exercises in a circuit around the gym. The exercises chosen should stress all parts of the body. These movements are performed with an absolute minimum of rest between exercises. Then at the end of a circuit, a rest interval of 2-5 minutes is taken before going through the circuit again. Three-five circuits would constitute a circuit-training program.

CLEAN

This movement consists of raising a barbell or two dumbbells from the floor to your shoulders in one smooth motion to prepare for an overhead lift. To properly execute a clean movement, you must use the coordinated strength of your legs, back, shoulders, and arms.

COLLAR

A clamp is used to hold plates securely in place on a barbell or dumbbell bar. The cylindrical metal clamps are held in place on the bar by means of a setscrew threaded through the collar and tightened securely against the bar. Inside collars keep plates from sliding inward and injuring your hands, while outside collars keep plates from sliding off the barbell in the middle of an exercise.

CUT UP (OR CUT)

A term used to denote a bodybuilder who has an extremely high degree of muscular definition due to a low degree of body fat.

DEFINITION

The absence of fat over clearly delineated muscular movement. Definition is often referred to as "muscularity," and a highly defined bodybuilder has so little body fat that very fine grooves of muscularity called "striations" will be clearly visible over each major muscle group.

DENSITY

This is the hardness of the muscle, which is also related to muscular definition. A bodybuilder can be well defined and still have excess fat within each major muscle complex. However, when he has muscle density, even this intramuscular fat has been eliminated. A combination of muscle mass and muscle density is highly prized among all competitive bodybuilders.

DIPPING BAR

Parallel bars set high enough above the floor to allow you to do dips between them, leg raises for your abdominal, and a variety of other exercises. Some gyms have dipping bars, which are angled inward at one end; these can be used when changing your grip width on dips.

DIURETICS

Sometimes called "water pills," these drugs and herbal preparations remove excess water from bodybuilder's system just prior to a show. This reveals greater muscular detail. Harsh chemical diuretics can be quite harmful to your health, particularly if they are used on a chronic basis. Two of the side effects of excessive chemical diuretic use are muscle cramps and heart arrhythmias (irregular heartbeats).

DUMBBELL

Essentially, a dumbbell is a short-handled barbell (usually 10-16 inches in length) intended primarily for use with one in each hand. Dumbbells are especially valuable when training the arms and shoulders, but can be used to build up almost any muscles.

EXERCISE

Movements such as a seated pulley row, barbell curl, bench press, or seated calf raise, etc that you perform in your workouts.

EZ-CURL BAR

A special type of barbell used in many arm exercises, but particularly for standing EZ-bar curls wherein it removes strain from your wrists. An EX-curl bar is also occasionally called a "cambered bar." Albert Beckles, one of the sport's most successful professionals from the 1980's, whimsically calls this piece of equipment a "wiggly bar" because of its shape.

FAILURE

That point in an exercise, which you have fully fatigued your working muscles. They can no longer complete an additional repetition of a movement with strict biomechanics. You should always take your post-warm-up sets at least to the point of momentary muscular failure, and frequently past that point.

FLEXIBILITY

A suppleness of joints, muscle masses, and connective tissues, which lets you, move your limbs over an exaggerated range of motion, a valuable quality in bodybuilding training, since it promotes optimum physical development. Flexibility can only be attained through systematic stretching training, which should form a cornerstone of your overall bodybuilding philosophy.

FORCED REPS

Forced reps are a frequently used method of extending a set past the point of failure to induce greater gains in muscle mass and quality. With forced reps, a training partner pulls upward on the bar just enough for you to grind out two or three reps past the failure threshold.

FORM

This is simply another word to indicate the biomechanics used during the performance of any bodybuilding or weight-training movement. Perfect form involves moving only the muscles specified in an exercise description, while moving the weight over the fullest possible range of motion.

FREE WEIGHTS

Equipment such as: Barbells, dumbbells, and related equipment. Serious bodybuilders use a combination of free weights and such exercise machines as those manufactured by Nautilus and Universal Gyms, but they primarily use free weights in their workouts.

GIANT SETS

Performing a series of 3-5 exercises, done with little or no rest between each movements, and a rest interval of 3-4 minutes between each giant sets. You can perform giant sets for either two antagonistic muscle groups or a single body part.

HYPERTROPHY

This means increase in muscle mass and an improvement in relative muscular strength. Placing an "over-load" on the working muscles with various training techniques during a bodybuilding workout induces hypertrophy.

IFBB

The International Federation of Bodybuilders, the gigantic sports federation founded in1946 by Joe and Ben Weider. With more than 120 member nations, the IFBB proves that bodybuilding is one of the most popular of all sports on the international level.

Through its member national federations, the IFBB oversees competitions in each nation, and it directly administers amateur and professional competition for men, women, and mixed pairs internationally.

INTENSITY

The degree of effort that you put into each set of your workout. The more intensity you place on a working muscle, the more quickly it will increase in hypertrophy. The most basic methods of increasing intensity are to use heavier weights in good form in each exercise, do more reps with a set weight, or perform a consistent number of sets and reps with a particular weight in a movement, but progressively reducing the length of rest intervals between sets.

ISOLATION EXERCISE

In contrast to a basic exercise, an isolation movement stresses a single muscle group (or sometimes just part of a single muscle) in relative isolation from the remainder of the body. Isolation exercises are good for shaping and defining various muscle groups. For your thighs: squats would be a typical basic movement. While leg extensions would be the equivalent isolation exercise.

JUICE

A slang term for anabolic steroids, e.g., being "on the juice."

LAYOFF

Most intelligent bodybuilders take a one or two-week layoff from bodybuilding training from time to time, during which they totally avoid the gym. A layoff after a period of intense pre-competition preparation is particularly beneficial as a means of allowing the body to completely rest, recuperate, and heal any minor training injuries that might have cropped up.

LIFTING BELT

This is a leather belt 3-5 inches wide at the back that is fastened tightly around your waist when you do squats, heavy back work, and overhead pressing movements. A lifting belt adds stability to your midsection, preventing lower back and abdominal injuries.

MASS

The size of the entire physique or the size of each muscle group. As long as you also have a high degree of muscularity and good balance of physical proportions, muscle mass is a highly prized quality among competitive bodybuilders.

MUSCULARITY

An alternative term for "definition" or "cuts."

NPC

The National Physique Committee Inc., which administers men's and women's amateur bodybuilding competitions in the United States. The NPC National Champions in each weight division are annually sent abroad to compete in the IFBB World Championships.

NUTRITION

The applied science of eating to foster greater health, fitness, and muscular grains. Through correct application of nutritional practices, you can selectively add muscle mass to your physique, or totally strip away all body fat, revealing the hard-earned muscles lying beneath your skin.

OLYMPIC BARBELL

A special type of barbell used in weightlifting and powerlifting competitions, but also used by bodybuilders in heavy basic exercises such as squats, bench presses, barbell be rows, standing barbell curls, standing barbell presses, and deadlifts. An Olympic barbell sans collars weighs 45 pounds, and each collar weighs five pounds.

OLYMPIC LIFTING

The type of weightlifting competition contested at the Olympic Games every four years, as well as at national and international competitions each year. Two lifts (the snatch and the clean jerk) are contested in a wide variety of weight classes.

OVERLOAD

The amount of weight that you force a muscle to use that is over and above its normal strength ability. Applying an overload to a muscle forces it to increase in hypertrophy.

PEAK

The absolute zenith of competitive condition achieved by a bodybuilder. To peak out optimally for a bodybuilding show, you must intelligently combine bodybuilding training, aerobic workouts, diet, mental conditioning, tanning, and a large number of other preparatory factors.

PLATES

The flat discs placed on the ends of barbell and dumbbell bars to increase the weight of the apparatus. Although some plates are made from vinyl-covered concrete, the best and most durable plates are manufactured from metal. Plates range in size from 1.25 - 100 pounds but using the term "plate" by itself refers to the 45 pounders.

POSE

Each individual stance that a bodybuilder does onstage in order to highlight his muscular development.

POUNDAGE

The amount of weight that you use in an exercise, whether that weight is on a barbell, dumbbell, or exercise machine.

POWER LIFTING

A second form of competitive weightlifting (not contested in the Olympics, however) featuring three lifts: The squat, bench press, and deadlift. Power lifting is contested both nationally and internationally in a wide variety of weight classes for both men and women.

PROGRESSION

The act of gradually adding to the amount of resistance that you use in each exercise. Without consistent progression in your workouts, you won't overload your muscles sufficiently to promote optimum increases in hypertrophy.

PUMP

The tight, blood-congested feeling in a muscle after it has been intensely trained. Muscle pump is caused by a rapid influx of blood into the muscles to remove fatigue toxins and replace supplies of fuel and oxygen. A good muscle pump is one of the indicators that show you have optimally worked a muscle group.

REPETITION (REP)

Each individual count of an exercise that is performed. Series of repetitions called "sets" are performed on each exercise in your training program.

RESISTANCE

The actual amount of weight that you are using in any exercise.

REST INTERVAL

The brief rest between sets that allows your body to partially recuperate prior to initiating the succeeding set. Usually between 1-5 minutes depending on how big the muscle group is.

RIPPED

The same as cut up.

ROUTINE

Also called a training schedule or program, a routine is the total list of exercise, sets, and reps (and sometimes weights) used in one training session.

SET

A grouping of repetitions that is followed by a rest interval and usually another set. Three to five sets are usually performed of each exercise.

SLEEVE

The hollow metal tube fit over the bar on most exercise barbell and dumbbell sets. This sleeve makes it easier for the bar to rotate in your hands as you do an exercise.

SPOTTERS

Training partners who stand by to act as safety helpers when you perform such heavy exercises as squats and bench presses. If you are stuck under and weight or begin to lose control of it, spotters can rescue you and prevent needless injuries.

STEROIDS

Prescription drugs which mimic male hormones, but without most of the androgenic side effects of actual testosterone. Many bodybuilders use these drugs to help increase muscle mass and strength.

STICKING POINT

A stalling out of bodybuilding progress. Also called a plateau.

STRETCHING

A type of exercise program in which you assume exaggerated postures that stretch muscles, joints, and connective tissues, hold these positions for several seconds, relax and then repeat the postures. Regular stretching exercise promotes body flexibility.

STRETCH MARKS

Tiny tears in a bodybuilder's skin caused by poor diet and in addition, rapid increases in bodyweight. If you notice stretch marks forming on your own body (usually around your pectoral-deltoid tie-ins), rub vitamin E cream over them two or three times per day, and try cutting back on your body weight by reducing body fat levels.

STRIATIONS

The tiny grooves of muscle across major muscle groups in a highly defined bodybuilder.

SUPERSETS

Series of two exercises performed with no rest between sets and a normal rest interval between supersets. Supersets increase training intensity by reducing the average length of rest interval between sets. They are also performed on the same muscle, not two different muscle groups.

SUPPLEMENTS

Concentrated vitamins, minerals, and proteins used by bodybuilders to improve the overall quality of their diets. Many bodybuilders believe that food supplements help to promote quality muscle growth.

SYMMETRY

The shape or general outline of a person's body, as when seen in silhouette. If you have good symmetry, you will have relatively wide shoulders, flaring lats, a small waist-hip structure, and generally small joints.

TESTOSTERONE

The male hormone primarily responsible for the maintenance of muscle mass and strength induced by heavy training. Testosterone is secondarily responsible for developing such secondary male sex characteristics as a deep voice, body hair, and male pattern baldness.

TRISETS

Series of three exercises performed with no rest between movements and a normal rest interval between trisets. Trisets increase training intensity by reducing the average length of rest interval between sets.

VASCULARITY

A prominence of veins and arteries over the muscles and beneath the skin of a sell-defined bodybuilder.

WARM-UP

The 5-15 minutes session of light calisthenics, aerobic exercise, and stretching taken prior to handling heavy bodybuilding training movements. A good warm-up helps to prevent injuries and actually allows you to get more out of your training than if you went into a workout cold.

WEIGHT

The same as Poundage or Resistance.

WEIGHTLIFTING

The competitive form of weight training in which each athlete attempts to lift as much as he can in well-defined exercises. Olympic lifting and power lifting are the two types of weightlifting competition.

WEIGHT TRAINING

An umbrella term used to categorize all acts of using resistance training. Weight training can be used to improve the body, rehabilitate injuries, improve sports conditioning, or as a competitive activity in terms of bodybuilding weightlifting.

WORKOUT

A bodybuilding or weight-training session.

###